Daughter of the Cult

A Memoir of
Family, Faith,
and Freedom

Doris Jones

CLAY BRIDGES
PRESS

Daughter of the Cult
A Memoir of Family, Faith, and Freedom

Published by Clay Bridges Press in Houston, TX
www.ClayBridgesPress.com

Unless otherwise indicated, scripture quotations are taken from (KJV) King James Version (KJV): King James Version, public domain.

ISBN: 978-1-68488-157-4
eISBN: 978-1-68488-158-1

Special Sales: Most Clay Bridges titles are available in special quantity discounts. Custom imprinting or excerpting can also be done to fit special needs. Contact Clay Bridges at Info@ClayBridgesPress.com

For my grandchildren,
Samantha, Athena, Kodiak, Milo, and Olive

Table of Contents

Prologue 1971 ix
Chapter 1: Connecticut 1946 1
Chapter 2 : Bible School 9
Chapter 3: Toilet Paper Tubes 13
Chapter 4: Christmas Buggy 19
Chapter 5: Glady 23
Chapter 6: Muriel 27
Chapter 7: Camp Meeting 31
Chapter 8: Holy Jumper 35
Chapter 9: Linda 39
Chapter 10: Heaven and Hell 43
Chapter 11: The Rumbling 47
Chapter 12: Leaving 51
Chapter 13: Trailer Park 55
Chapter 14: The House 61
Chapter 15: Canvassers 65
Chapter 16: Stop! 69
Chapter 17: Night Vigil 73
Chapter 18: Easter 79
Chapter 19: Floydie 81
Chapter 20: The Visit 87
Chapter 21: Summer Days 91
Chapter 22: Convention 95
Chapter 23: Eighth Grade 99
Chapter 24: Work 105
Chapter 25: High School 109
Chapter 26: Senior Year 117
Chapter 27: Choosing 123
Chapter 28: South Chicago 129
Chapter 29: Back to Union Grove 133

Chapter 30: English 101 139
Chapter 31: Grandma 141
Chapter 32: Kicking Rocks 145
Chapter 33: Classes 149
Chapter 34: Looking Around 155
Chapter 35: Icy Roof 157
Chapter 36: More Classes 159
Chapter 37: Trapped 163
Chapter 38: Unplanned 167
Chapter 39: Hug 171
Chapter 40: To Connecticut 175
Chapter 41: Job Corps 181
Chapter 42: Next New Plan 187
Chapter 43: Betrayal 191
Chapter 44: Fasting and Praying 197
Chapter 45: Starting College 201
Chapter 46: Weekends 203
Chapter 47: Flat Tire 207
Chapter 48: Career Change 213
Chapter 49: The Big Mistake 217
Chapter 50: Moving On 227
Chapter 51: Virginia 233
Chapter 52: Indianapolis 237
Chapter 53: Taking Control 243
Chapter 54: Board Meeting 247
Chapter 55: Walking Out 251
Chapter 56: Tasting Freedom 255
Chapter 57: Equal Opportunity Act 259
Chapter 58: Ebbie Road 263
Chapter 59: Summer Job 265
Chapter 60: Mrs. Murray 267
Chapter 61: Found! 271
Epilogue 277
About the Author 285
Discussion Questions 287

Special Thanks

I want to thank my husband, Larry, for his patience and steady support throughout this journey. My son, Sam, has been an enthusiastic supporter, cheering me on from the start. My daughter, Sara, gave countless hours reading drafts with care. My daughter-in-law, Tara, read with insight and encouraged me when I needed it most. I am deeply grateful to my niece Grace for her thoughtful editing and to my niece Mae for her encouragement.

Special thanks also go to my book coach and the dedicated staff at Lucid Books for their guidance and patience. This book could not have come to life without each of you.

Prologue 1971

It was a week after Thanksgiving in 1971. My thirtieth birthday had fallen around the holiday. Maybe it was that milestone that brought on my ultimatum, but it probably would've happened anyway. Something had to change.

I'd made a terrible mistake coming back to this church school in Potomac, Illinois, and I was paying for it every day. I'd been so eager to share the wonders of science I had discovered in college that I hadn't counted the cost—the cost of watching *him* perform day after day on a false stage.

It was a Friday afternoon. I stood in my classroom, preparing to close it down before the weekend. A faint metallic odor still lingered in the air as I placed the last beakers and graduated cylinders on the shelf and shut the windows. It was cold outside, but during experiments I liked the ventilation.

My four high school chemistry students had heated rust and charcoal—technically iron oxide and carbon. The smell came mostly from the gas flames they used to melt the compounds.

I'd seen the excitement in their eyes as they watched the mixture bubble and fuse into a dark clump.

Because I also taught biology, my classroom had a microscope. We carefully scraped tiny splinters of the cooled lump onto a glass slide. When the students saw the sparkling silver fragments of reconstructed iron glint under the lens, I was reminded of how much I love teaching. I was in the right profession. I just wasn't in the right place.

I walked the length of the gas-line contraption that bisected my room, checking each shutoff valve. It was the church handyman's project—functional, but I wasn't sure it would pass a proper safety inspection.

Everything at that small church boarding school had been built with love and a prayer. I graduated from high school there thirteen years ago and then was immediately catapulted into the church as a dedicated worker—canvassers we were called who went door-to-door sharing about the church and selling Christian literature. When I was twenty-one, I started teaching there with only a high school diploma. That would last four years. Now I was back again, this time with a brand-new college degree.

I pulled the classroom door shut with a soft click and passed a few teachers who were still at their desks shuffling papers. I'd been administering Friday tests part of the day, giving myself time to think through what I needed to say. Now it was time.

I headed for the door marked "Principal." I knocked once and walked in. He was about to leave. The light was off, and the weak rays of the winter sun barely pierced the gloom of his small office. When he saw me, I noticed something shift—a tightness in his lips, a drooping of his shoulders. At forty-nine, the man in front of me looked old and worn out.

It always shocked me to see that the spark was gone from his eyes. Maybe others hadn't noticed, but I could see that our adversarial stance had left him hollowed out, like a lamp with no fuel.

We'd had this conversation before, but today, something in me cracked wide open. My anger had built until the fuse finally met the dynamite. I was furious—with him, yes, but also with myself for staying silent so long in this world of lies. He might be able to live with the burden. I could not.

I had watched my parents suffer under the weight of this church for many years. My sister Gloria was slowly sinking in despair because her family's needs were not being met there. How could I go on teaching, praying, and pretending when I held onto a truth that would destroy everything?

The last time the principal and I spoke, he had looked me in the eyes and warned me: If I ever told anyone, he'd go to my father with a story that would "send him to his grave." But I knew better. For all my father's rashness, he wouldn't be swayed by a man who was calling his daughter unstable. He wouldn't buy it. My father was still boasting to anyone who would listen that I was the only one of his six children who had graduated from college, and *summa cum laude* at that.

I faced my nemesis. "You have to fix this," I said, struggling to control myself. Fixing it had become my mantra.

He began edging toward the door. I moved to block him.

"This time, you're going to hear me." I threw my words like stones. "You know what this is about. How can you keep pretending? You have to do something. You counsel these kids, you preach, you stand there like everything is fine, but it's not! I'm dying inside just watching the show you put on."

My voice was loud. "I keep telling you that I can't fix things, but you *can*. Just be honest. You have to fix it." I was shaking with the effort to hold back tears. "I didn't know it would be like this when I came back after college."

It felt like I was pouring my soul out to a statue—a crumbling, deaf, and blind statue. My tears fell. His eyes glazed.

"Someone's going to hear you," he whispered.

I responded more loudly, stepping into his space. "Maybe you'd be happy if I just disappeared. You'd tell everyone you didn't see it coming. You'd tell my family I lost my mind. You think I won't do something desperate?"

My fists clenched. The threat was out. I was at a breaking point.

He slipped around me, opened the door, and was gone.

I ran after him. His truck was backed up near the building. As he reached for the door handle, I darted in front of the hood, arms wide, daring him. My cheeks burned as the biting cold wind whipped against my face. I was shaking.

He climbed into the cab and slammed the door. I didn't move. We locked eyes through the windshield, my gaze full of rage and desperation. A student appeared at the bottom of the hill, heading our way. I lowered my arms. Slowly, I stepped aside. The truck engine revved, and he was gone.

Chapter 1
Connecticut 1946

My parents named me Doris, after my mother because I was born on her birthday, November 27, 1941. I grew up with the nickname Dorie, but with my New England accent, I would tell you my name was "Dari."

My brother Floydie was my playmate; he was seven years older. Sometimes he teased me until I cried. He kept me in a state of fright with his talk of the war, repeating what he heard from kids at his one-room school. My mother told him not to scare me, but I knew all about blackouts and bombs.

I wouldn't go into the chicken coop with Floydie anymore to gather eggs after the time he told me to reach under a setting hen. She flew up, wings whirring, toes curled, beady eyes glaring, and a sharp yellow beak open in fury. Even my brother ran away from her.

I played under the peach trees, stuffing ripe peaches into my fiver-year-old mouth until the juice ran down my chin and soaked the bib of my sunsuit. As shadows lengthened, I always watched for my father's green 1940 Pontiac that came slowly up the rutted dirt lane every evening. I would run along behind it and then dance up and down when he stopped, opened the car door, and reached for his black lunch bucket. As usual, he opened his bucket and pretended to be surprised at the little corner of his sandwich that he pulled out and gave to me. I chewed the dry bread and followed him into the house.

Linda, my little sister, was usually on the floor at my mother's feet. She couldn't come outside to play with us unless my mother watched her because her lips would turn blue and she'd topple over if she ran. Her little front teeth were gray. My mother said it was from hitting her face on the ground too many times.

I was aware that changes were coming to our family. I didn't know these were the last days my father would be working at Electric Boat in Groton, Connecticut. I knew the war was finally over, but how could I know that worse terrors were coming? I didn't know yet about hell. When aunts and uncles dropped by, I started hearing about a man named Mr. Hitchcock.

My father talked about a Bible School—a church-run boarding school in Waukesha, Wisconsin. I knew about that school because my three older sisters had gone away to high school there. A different sister each year would stay home in Connecticut to help my mother.

Glady, the oldest, was nineteen now. Gloria was eighteen, and Muriel was seventeen. Muriel had just graduated from the school that spring, and now all of them were working for the church that ran the Bible School.

Many years later, in one of only two letters I ever received from my father's mother, Grandmother Phoebe, she wrote that I had once told her, "We are going a long way off, but I will be back to see you." I never saw her again. She and my grandfather had spent most of their lives at the Bible School and working for the church in Waukesha. But after the Depression when the Bible School didn't need them any longer, they ended up back in Connecticut.

Mr. Hitchcock wrote to my father in Connecticut that spring and suggested he sell the house and move his family to the Bible

School in Waukesha. They could be closer to their daughters—Glady, Gloria, and Muriel—who were working for the church and could not go home to Connecticut. All of a sudden, new furniture began appearing in our house: a blue chair with wooden arms, a new desk, a big wooden bed my mother said was maple, and a mattress we were not allowed to jump on. A matching dresser with a round mirror and a tall chiffonier with drawers finished out the set. This was the first new furniture my mother had ever owned. We walked carefully around it. And what was the reason for all the new furniture? Was my father giving my mother nice things so she would agree to leave Connecticut and move to Waukesha, Wisconsin?

On a hot summer day that year in 1946 when I was four, we were on our way to Wisconsin, to the Bible School run by the Metropolitan Church Association. My father drove my mother, my little sister Linda, and me to Grand Central Station in New York City. My mother had said her final goodbyes to the old farmhouse in Quakertown, Connecticut, where she was born, and to her parents now resting in the cemetery down the road. My father was born in Quakertown as well, but he had grown up at the Bible School.

After a long wait in Grand Central Station, we stepped out to where the trains were waiting. The reverberation of the hot air, the screeching locomotive wheels, and the hissing steam seemed to lift me off my feet. I grabbed my father's hand with both of mine and stumbled along the uneven brick pavement. People ran past, some dragging trunks and some soldiers still in their battle uniforms. Shoes, boots, and bags swirled around me until finally I saw the conductor in his gold and blue uniform standing by the open door of the coach.

My mother climbed the steps, lifting and pushing Linda in front of her. She turned and reached for the suitcase my father was carrying, and then he boosted me up the steps. I clutched a fistful of his shirt as if this were a last goodbye. He would not be coming with us on the train. He and my brother Floydie would follow later in the car, pulling a trailer filled with my mother's new furniture. He pried my hand loose, and I climbed the steps behind my mother into the women's coach.

We found our way to an empty seat that was wide enough for two passengers. I pushed up against the window while Linda squirmed for a spot beside me. The other seats were already filling with women fanning their faces and trying to chase away the stifling heat and the fumes from burning coal. Everything we touched was grimy with soot. I ran my fingers across the window. My mother reached for my hand, but the train jolted and swayed, and she had to grab Linda instead.

We were moving now, out of the tunnel, past tall buildings and busy streets, and into green farmland that slowly came into focus through the smoky window. I gazed at hills dotted with animals like our old workhorse, Lady. My brother would hitch her up to the express wagon and haul loads of wood he helped my father cut on our farm. They used a two-man saw that was taller than I was. I still had a scar on my wrist that looked just like a V from a tooth of that saw. I remembered the scolding I got for playing hide-and-seek and choosing the wrong hiding place— the corner of the porch where the saw leaned against the wall.

I was seeing black-and-white cows now for the first time. Our cow at home was a brown Guernsey, and my mother always said a Guernsey gave the richest milk with the most cream.

The bread we ate for supper on the train that night was from the loaves my mother baked every week. The butter came from the cream she churned, and the sweet jam was the result of hours she spent over the stove preserving the strawberries from our garden.

The train chugged on, swaying and belching smoke. Linda sat on my mother's lap, and in a moment of daring, I slipped into the aisle, stumbling and catching myself as I adjusted to the movement of the train. As I made my way between the rows of seats, a woman who was peeling an orange gave me two juicy sections. I carried them back in my grubby hands to share with Linda, the sweet smell of fruit overpowering the smell of the burning coal.

It must have been a long night for my mother as she shifted my sleeping sister on the seat beside her, smoothing her red hair that was wet with sweat. The window was lowered to let in the cool night breeze, but every time the train slowed for a crossing or a town, a sharp whistle pierced the silence in the coach. I was stretched out on the floor, using my mother's feet for a pillow. The rhythmic rumbling of the train lulled me, but the clacking of the wheels echoed in my dreams.

My mother's thoughts must have drifted back to the time she had once lived at the Bible School when my older sisters were young. My father had spent much of his childhood there, until he was nineteen when his parents left the Bible School and returned to Connecticut. My grandfather had been a farmer before they joined the church in 1904. They were farming again when my father met my mother.

In 1925, four years and three babies after my parents married in the chapel on a ledge in Quakertown, my father's older brother died after a short illness. My mother wrote, "This changed everything." My father's mother believed God was punishing them for leaving the church and insisted that all her remaining children go back to the Bible School. My grandparents sold their farm in Connecticut and rejoined the Metropolitan Church. My father took his wife and three young children to Waukesha and began to follow church orders.

Thirteen years later as the Great Depression was in full swing, the devastating hurricane of 1938 hit New England. After hearing that my mother's parents were surviving with half their roof blown off, windows shattered, and one chimney toppled, my father spoke:

"I think we should go help your folks." Anyone who did not follow the orders of the leader of the Metropolitan Church Association lost their ticket to heaven, so my family left the church as sinners and went to help my mother's folks in Quakertown, Connecticut.

After spending nearly all her married life following my father's family in the church, my mother was finally home again. She was back in the familiar farmhouse where she was born among the grey stone ledges covered with moss and lichens. They were the stone walls of her girlhood with the chapel on the ledge that her grandfather had built when there was no church building in Quakertown.

My father pruned the apple and peach trees that still stood after the storm, and the old-fashioned pink roses bloomed around the kitchen stoop. The house had been there since the late 1790s, and now my mother's parents gave it to our family in exchange for caring for them during this difficult time. My father repaired the roof, replaced the windows, and rebuilt the chimney.

One of the first things he did after the essential repairs was to have an electric wire run to the house and a pump installed to bring water from the well to the kitchen sink. My grandfather would stand and pull on the string from the ceiling, turning the light bulb on and off and shaking his head in wonder. Then he'd stand at the sink watching the cold water flow and say, "Pshaw, I don't know why that little tank don't run dry."

On the train that night, my mother's sleep must have been interrupted time and again with memories of that farm. Selling the farm and moving to Wisconsin weighed heavily on her. What if the older girls were not happy working for the church and wanted to come home? There would be no home for them in Connecticut. Was this the right move for Floydie—leaving the life where he had thrived? Linda might be better off with Christian people around her to pray. Sturdy little Dorie (me) would be happy wherever her mother was.

The sun was shining when I awoke on the train floor. Women were taking turns in the restroom at the front of the coach, preparing for arrival in Chicago. My mother ushered Linda and me down the aisle into the small restroom. She scrubbed the soot and grime from our faces and hands, and changed us into matching yellow sundresses. My big sister Gloria was waiting for us at Union Station in Chicago.

Then there was the blur of a long car trip, a big building, a noisy room where we ate supper, and finally settling into our cots that night. "Sweet dreams. I'll go to breakfast in the morning and bring yours when I come back." My mother kissed us goodnight.

Chapter 2
Bible School

"Mama forgot us!"

I jumped off my cot and ran over to Linda's cot, grabbing her sheet. We were in a large, empty room except for a suitcase and the cots where we slept. We had arrived last night after a long train ride and car ride, and now we were a thousand miles from home. It was summer, and two wide windows along the wall streamed in bright sunlight.

Linda started to wail. She was only three.

"Hurry, get up, we have to go find Mama," I said as I pulled on her little arms and legs until she sat up.

Our clothes from the day before were in a messy pile on the floor, our shoes beside them. Just yesterday we had been sparkly clean and pretty in our matching yellow dresses when our sister Gloria met us at the train in Chicago. I knew we were now at the Bible School, but the train ride, the car ride, Daddy, and my brother Floydie were all mixed up with my dreams.

I grabbed my yellow dress, now grubby and limp. It buttoned in the back with a long sash on each side that my mother always tied into a bow. I was four and a half and gave up quickly with the buttons. We had slept in our petticoats, so I pulled Linda's dress over her head and turned her around. She was still wailing.

I scuffed into my unbuckled brown shoes and picked up Linda's white high-tops. She still wore baby shoes, though her third birthday had been last week. I left the laces hanging and grabbed her hand.

My first challenge was getting out of the room. There were three doors. One was opposite the windows and had a large glass transom above it. That door was locked. I pulled Linda through a door that was slightly ajar on the side of the room. We entered a room I remembered from the night before—the big table, another cot, and my mother's words that this bed was for my brother. He was coming later with my father and my mother's new furniture.

I opened another door and saw a long, dark hallway with doors along either side as far as I could see. We were at one end. Heading out, I noticed that this main door was enormous. It must have been slightly ajar. I had never seen a door handle with a thumb latch before. We stumbled into a large entry space, and just in front of us was a staircase leading up.

I dragged Linda upstairs and stopped in confusion. We were in a huge, old building. It had been built in 1887 as a luxury spa hotel in Waukesha, Wisconsin, known as the Fountain Spring House. Now it was the Bible School that belonged to the Metropolitan Church Association. It covered an entire city block and had 450 rooms and two dining rooms that could seat 800.

We entered a long hallway, this one carpeted and lit by lamps along the walls. Closed doors lined both sides. In the distance, I could hear the clatter of dishes and the hum of voices. We followed the noise. Ahead, light was spilling into the hallway.

I gripped Linda's hand and stepped into a large room. I didn't register the shiny, polished wood floors or the long rows of tables with white linen tablecloths at eye level. But I did notice the people, more than I had ever seen in one room.

An abrupt silence fell, and nearly a hundred pairs of eyes turned toward us.

There we stood, our dirty dresses unbuttoned, sashes trailing, hair uncombed, and shoes scuffed. And then, piercing the stillness, Linda let out a scream.

Suddenly, our mother was running down the center aisle from the very back of the room. We ran to her, meeting in the middle of the dining hall. She bent and gathered us in with a hug and picked up Linda. With me clutching her skirt, she walked us back down the big hall, down the stairs, through the entryway, and into the dark hall to the three-room suite that was now our new home.

My mother reminded me that she had told us she would go to breakfast and bring something back for us to eat. She never dreamed that after our long trip on the train I would awaken before she returned. She was getting clean dresses out of the suitcase when my sister Gloria came in. She carried a tray with two bowls of cornflakes and a pitcher of milk. We sat down at the table in our kitchen to eat our breakfast.

"When are we going home?" I asked.

Chapter 3
Toilet Paper Tubes

Soon I was adjusting to our new life at the Bible School. We had three rooms in what was called the school "el." It was on the ground floor, only a few steps from the play yard.

The play yard was my happy place. There were tall steel frames with six swings. I could stand and pump, sit and pump, and play in the deep mud puddles under the swings when it rained. There were teeter-totters, but we didn't use them much. Linda was so tiny that when we tried, she hung in the air and screamed while I was stuck on the ground. There were monkey bars, which I grew into, and a merry-go-round with long, tangled chains. And there was the sandbox where I played for hours. Old grey boards around the edge held the sand as deep as I could dig. escape.

This was the life my father brought us into, but it became the box from which I could not I didn't begin to seriously wonder why my parents took our family back to the Bible School until after my father died. My sister Muriel thought it might have been because there was no Metropolitan Church in Quakertown, Connecticut.

My mother said it was because the Bible School felt more like home to him. Gloria said it was the letter from Mr. Hitchcock.

Many years later, I was sitting beside my Uncle Chauncey, my father's youngest brother, at his ninetieth birthday party. Some of the old-timers from the Bible School had come to celebrate with him. I asked my uncle why my father had taken us back to the Bible School that summer after the war. He looked at me and paused. He had worked for the church as a missionary and had wrestled with it in prayer throughout the years. With old eyes and sorrow in his voice, he spoke softly: "I don't think he knew. I don't think he knew it was a cult."

A few weeks after we arrived at the Bible School, I started school—public school—for the first time. I went to afternoon kindergarten wearing my blue sweater, the one Grandma Phoebe in Connecticut had knit for me.

"Just like October's bright blue weather," my mother said, watching me cross Grand Avenue on my way to school. I looked over my shoulder. My mother and Linda were waving. I would be five in a few months, and public school was just another new thing in my new life.

It was a city school, noisy and crowded, so different from the one-room elementary schoolhouse in Quakertown where my older siblings had gone and where I would have gone. I stood alone on the playground in a dress my mother had sewn back in Connecticut. I watched a little girl in a golden plaid dress and hair with short curls that matched. She was laughing, surrounded by other little girls who looked just like her. I didn't know how to join them. I didn't know how to belong.

After school, on the walk back to the Bible School, a boy across the street kept pace with me, chanting "freckle-face" over and over. By the time I reached our rooms, I was crying big, aching tears. My mother tried to comfort me, but I was on the verge of realizing that I didn't fit in and that bullies would be part of my world from now on.

Inside my school one day, I heard more whispering than usual—a lot more. Something exciting was about to happen. And then our teacher said it: "Doris, you and Maxine did not bring a tube, so you may go to the little table in the corner."

I felt my lips tremble and my chin quiver as I hung my head and crept into the corner.

The teacher gave each of us a piece of paper and set a box of crayons on the table.

I lifted my head and glared at the little girl across from me. I wasn't angry at her. I wouldn't have even known her name if the teacher hadn't called us out together. But sharing my shame was too big a feeling for an almost five-year-old.

I tried not to look out into the room, but I couldn't help myself. Everyone had a little gray tube. So that's what the teacher had meant when she asked us to bring a toilet paper tube.

I watched her pass out small scissors. My eyes widened when I saw the pieces of black and orange tissue paper on each desk. Then the teacher brought out the big white jar of paste, and each student came up to get a dab. I listened to the chatter, the crinkling of paper. I smelled the sweetness of the paste.

Worst of all, after school I trailed behind as everyone ran ahead, tooting their little orange and black horns, honking and jamming up the hill. I saw Maxine wiping her nose.

That night, I checked the bathroom in our rooms again. I had looked before, but this time I knelt down and studied the little black box beside the toilet. I opened the lid. It was full of folded white tissue papers. I felt along the bottom. There was a slit where we pulled the paper out. There was no tube.

I didn't know about Halloween. I didn't know about toilet paper tubes. What else was I missing? I stood with a wrinkly scowl on my forehead. The bathtub loomed in front of me, taking up one wall. I ran my hand along its curling edge, cold and smooth on my fingertips.

In Connecticut, bath time had been in the kitchen. My mother would tell my brother to fetch kindling to heat the water in the reservoir on the back of the stove. Then she'd bring out the round, galvanized tub. Linda and I would climb in together, knees touching, as our mother poured warm water around us.

This new white clawfoot bathtub was so big that we could both lie down in it at the same time. I had not yet forgotten my farmhouse life. Old and new were fighting for space in my mind.

We'd lived in a farmhouse in Connecticut with an upstairs, but here in the Bible School, the stairs went on forever, and there were hundreds of rooms. Each room had a door with a glass transom. In our three-room suite, we used only the door in the middle room to enter and exit.

Linda and I slept in the big room with our parents and my mother's maple bed and matching chest that our father had hauled in the trailer. The mirror had made the trip safely. The rich golden glow of the maple furniture reminded me of my mother's bargain. This new furniture was her price for returning to the Bible School in Waukesha, Wisconsin.

Linda's cot was in the corner; mine was on the opposite wall. Linda had decorated the wallpaper beside her bed with red crayon. I could never look at the scribbles without getting upset.

In front of one big window stood my mother's treadle sewing machine. She could sew while watching us in the play yard. A little red table and two small chairs sat in front of the other window.

The middle room, our kitchen, had a big brown table and four chairs. A tall wooden pantry lined one wall. But the kitchen was missing the most important things—a stove and an icebox. My mother never cooked during our time at the Bible School. She kept cereal and milk for breakfast, and there were always graham crackers.

The bathroom was off the kitchen. The third room, our parlor, was closest to the outside door. Its windows looked out on the sandbox. My mother's blue chair and desk were in there, along with a couch and a piano.

When my father and brother had arrived with the furniture, my brother whispered to me that he saw Daddy hand over the Pontiac keys to the man who managed the church fleet. The car wasn't all he gave away. After buying my mother's furniture, he handed over to the church the rest of the money from the sale of our farm. We lived by this scripture: "But my God will supply all your need according to His riches in glory by Christ Jesus" (Phil. 4:19).

Chapter 4
Christmas Buggy

Christmas at the Bible School was always happy. My father would cut a tree from one of the church farms and my mother would string bubble lights she brought from Connecticut, plastic stars, and glittery gold angels hanging on tiny threads. We also had a box of glass balls, each wrapped in tissue paper. Every year, there was more empty tissue and fewer glass balls, despite the warnings to be careful.

We were never disappointed in our gifts. With no catalogues, stores, or friends with toys, we relied on our mother to suggest what we should ask for and it was Jesus, not Santa Claus, who we asked. Our prayers were always answered. That first Christmas we must have been praying for a doll buggy.

That first Christmas at the Bible School, my mother had no money for gifts. Sometimes someone would give her a dollar or two, but not that year. She often told the story of how God answered her prayers as she worried about Christmas morning. One day when she was outside, she saw Mr. Herbert, the junk man, park in the back of the building with his truck overflowing.

He drove through the affluent neighborhoods on trash day, collecting anything that could be repaired or broken down for parts. My mother spotted an old doll carriage and hurried over to ask for it. “I had your girls in mind,” he said, climbing up to the top of the truck and carefully bringing it down.

The carriage, what my mother called a buggy, was made of woven wicker. All the wheels were intact, but the handlebar was broken. It had been loved hard, and the inside cloth was torn away. My mother carried it down to the carpenter’s shop in the basement where he patched it up and crafter a new wooden handle painted black.

My mother rewove the wicker and painted the buggy green with yellow trim and yellow- and-black wheels. She made a cozy interior with fuzzy brown flannel. The buggy looked like new with little plastic windows in the folding hood. She even sewed a doll blanket with red and pink roses.

On Christmas Eve, excitement built. Only my father, mother, Floydie, Linda, and I were there. My three older sisters were working for the church—Glady and Gloria in the Chicago location and Muriel in Cincinnati. Though they weren’t too far away, they were not allowed to come home. Most of the older workers were from the church orphanage and didn’t have families. Others, like my sisters, came from the church high school. If they went home for Christmas, the church feared they would not return.

Early Christmas morning, my mother opened the parlor door. The corner with the Christmas tree dazzled with bubble lights and shiny glass balls. Then Linda and I saw the buggy. At first, we just stood there, staring in wonder. Then we ran to it and stopped. We looked at our mother. Were we allowed to touch it?

Two beautiful dolls sat in the buggy. Our oldest sister, Glady, had saved her small allowance and bought them for us. They wore silky dresses with layers of ruffles. My doll’s dress was blue and white, and Linda’s was the same pattern in red and white. We had never seen dolls like these. We had rag dolls made by our grandmother, but nothing so exquisite and elegant had ever entered our world of dreams.

The dolls' bodies were stuffed cloth, but their arms and legs were made of molded plaster-like material. Their hollow heads were painted with big blue eyes and brown hair.

I named my doll Ellen, and Linda called hers Betty. We played with that buggy all the years of my growing up until I left for boarding school when I was twelve.

Linda dropped her doll a few weeks after Christmas, and my mother found us trying to put the broken pieces of Betty's head back together. We both cried as our mother gently took the broken doll and put her away on the closet shelf.

We ate Christmas dinner at our table in the back of the dining room, closest to the swinging doors that led in and out of the kitchen. The waitresses were high school girls in white dresses and matching half-aprons, a different color each day. My favorites were the pink ones with frilly ruffles around the edges and a big starched bow in the back.

Later, when my sister Gloria was in charge of the waitresses, I stood in the kitchen watching the girls line up behind the doors, waiting for the prayer and then for everyone to sit down. One girl was assigned to Mr. Hitchcock's table. She was at the head of the line carrying steaming bowls of hot food. Mr. Hitchcock, the church leader, always sat at the first table inside the entrance. My mother said he always got real cream for his coffee.

Across the aisle from his table at the front of the room was a piano and a stage where music sometimes accompanied the meal. But we couldn't hear it very well. The exit door to the pot room was right behind our table, and all we heard was the banging and clatter of metal.

Linda sat in her highchair as far away from me as possible. My mother sat next to her. I sat at one corner with my father beside me on the left. In between were grownups who carried on conversations with my parents. I never talked, but I listened. Sometimes I had questions for my father after the meal.

"Were there really orphans here?" I asked.

"Yes," he replied. "There were over two hundred."

"Were you an orphan?"

"No, of course not," he said.

He told me how Grandma and Grandpa went to Chicago—the church's first headquarters before it moved to Waukesha—to help the church when he was just a baby. There were hundreds of poor people who had come to America and lived in tenements in Chicago with no toilets and no food. The church had so many orphans to take care of that they bought the Bible School in Waukesha, Wisconsin. Then Grandma and Grandpa went there to help take care of the orphans.

"Where did you live?"

I was surprised to learn that my father was four years old, just like me, when he moved to Waukesha, which became the church headquarters and also the location of the church's Bible School. He went to school with the orphans in the same hall where we now lived.

Chapter 5
Glady

Sunday dinner was always special. We had roast meat, potatoes with gravy, and cake or pie. At the end of the meal, a whispered message would pass from table to table, and the chatter would stop. Someone would rise and give the dismissal prayer. Then every chair would scrape the floor as talking resumed.

After Sunday dinner, stacks of the weekly *Burning Bush* magazine lay out to be distributed. I had heard the story about my grandparents and the *Burning Bush*.

In Connecticut, a butcher had used a page from the *Burning Bush* to wrap a piece of meat. After unwrapping it, an evangelist read the article and told my grandparents about the Christian work in Chicago. That was how they decided to join the Metropolitan Church.

One Sunday, my father picked up his copy as usual. It was a spring day. We fell into our routine, my mother taking Linda to the bedroom for her nap and I settling with my father in the parlor. I rested at one end of the couch, waiting for him to finish skimming the articles in the *Burning Bush*. The children's story was always on the last page.

He was mid-sentence, reading aloud, when a knock came on the door of the middle room.

No one ever visited on Sunday afternoon. My father jumped up, and I trailed closely behind.

I peeked around him as he opened the door. It was Glady, my oldest sister who had given me Ellen the doll that I played with every day. She saw me, and I smiled up at her. As I tried to squeeze past my father, the door slammed shut in my face.

There was one thing I could give her to show how much I loved the doll she'd given me. I had a fancy little plastic pin I wore on my dress. It was the size of a quarter, a blue bonnet with a pink daisy on the rim, tied with a soft blue ribbon. If I wasn't wearing it, I kept it in the top dresser drawer.

I burst into the bedroom where Linda was sleeping.

"Glady's here!" I shouted.

My mother looked up from her reading by the window. I yanked open the drawer, grabbed the pin, and ran into the hall. But Glady and my father weren't there.

Then I heard my father's voice. I pushed open the big door that led to the entry of the main building. Glady was halfway up the stairs and my father was below her, his arm outstretched. "Get out!" he bellowed. "Never come back!"

"Glady!" I called up to her. She turned and saw me just as I tried to dart past my father, holding out my little blue pin. He grabbed me roughly as she turned and ran farther up the stairs. "I never want to see you again!" he shouted after her. "You are no longer part of this family!" Then she was gone.

I clutched the little pin in my fist as my father ushered me down the stairs and back into our rooms. Linda was awake, but I never told her what I'd seen. I would be nineteen before I saw Glady again. She was gone. The fracture in our family was just beginning.

I went into the bedroom and picked up my doll, Ellen. I gently stroked her silky blue-and- white dress. I was tying the ribbons at the back of her neck when I heard a noise.

Linda had dragged our two little red chairs to the closet and stacked them, one on top of the other. There she stood, wobbling on the crooked top chair, stretching her thin little arms as high as she could to reach the shelf where my mother had placed her broken doll, Betty.

"Mama!" I screamed.

Mama came running. Lifting Linda down, she hugged her tightly. "I'm so sorry, honey," she said softly, "but I can't fix her. She's broken."

I looked at my doll one more time and then put Ellen away.

Chapter 6
Muriel

It was an early Friday morning in summer. I clutched my mother's hand as we walked across the back parking lot behind the Bible School. In my free hand, I carried a cloth bag with my nightgown, clean clothes, and books. I skipped and swung my bag. This was an important trip, to cheer up my sister Muriel. My mother told me I was just the one to do it because Muriel loved me so much. I tried to remember her. She was nineteen now and working in one of the church homes.

As my mother and I stepped into the early morning sunshine, a shiny black car was waiting. My mother told me I was going with Mr. and Mrs. Babel. Mr. Babel was driving, and his wife sat in the front passenger seat. I knew Mr. and Mrs. Babel by sight. I asked my mother two questions about almost everyone at the Bible School, especially if they were a Mr. and Mrs. "Do they have children?" I would always ask. I was surprised that God had not given out more babies. There were only two children in the Bible School besides us, little girls who lived with their grandmother on the third floor. The second question was always, "Are they saved and sanctified?" All the old people in the church were saved and sanctified, the rest of the people, maybe or maybe not. The Babels were definitely saved and sanctified. I couldn't remember if they had children, but they were the grandma-grandpa type.

My mother told me it was a long ride to Cincinnati where Muriel worked for the church. I wouldn't see my sister until nighttime. "Be a good girl," my mother said as she hugged me. I climbed into the back of the car and carefully laid my bag on the seat beside me. I watched my mother slam the door.

I looked back as we turned onto the road, but my mother was already gone. I was soon standing up on the floorboard in the back, leaning over the front seat to see better out the big window. This was my first car ride since leaving Connecticut a year ago. As the day wore on, I settled back with the two books from my bag. They were the only books I had that were just mine, with my name written inside the cover. They had colored pictures on every page. I knew all the words from my mother reading them to us so many times. I selected *Henry's Wagon*, and as I turned it right side up, I opened the back cover. I knew exactly what I would find, and for a moment my emotions tangled and twisted before I shut it again. Linda had taken my book, this one with my name inside, and scribbled in it with a pink crayon. My mother had stopped her before she could color the pages, but I had to look at her circles and loops every time I read my book.

I didn't bring my favorite book because it belonged to Linda and me together. It was a tall, narrow book with fairy tales and colored pictures. As we drove on and on that day with trees on both sides of the road, I imagined I was Little Red Riding Hood. When the tree branches touched overhead and made a leafy green tunnel, I stood on the floor in the middle of the car, jumping up and down.

We finally arrived in Cincinnati, Ohio. My mother was right. Muriel was really happy to see me. There were several women who lived in the house, but my sister took me upstairs to her room.

Outside her window, cars never stopped going up and down the street. The ladies in the house had no children, and I would learn later about canvassing, how church workers lived together and went door to door selling Christian literature day after day to support the church.

On Saturday, two women and Muriel took me to the zoo, or almost took me to the zoo. It was not open that day, or it cost too much to get in, I never knew which. We had walked past a carousel with horses dancing up and down and twirling around. I heard the music again as we walked back, and I tugged on my sister's hand.

"How much does it cost?" I whispered, pulling her off the sidewalk into the grass. "I think it's a nickel," she answered.

I wished with all my heart that someone had a nickel, and I learned that day that a nickel was an awfully lot of money.

That night, we sat at her window counting cars—blue ones for me and red ones for her.

She smiled at me, but her eyes were sad, and her voice seemed far away. I had come on a mission to cheer her up, but I knew I was failing. I didn't yet understand what weighed on her heart. I only sensed that something wasn't right. I would learn much later that Muriel was wrestling with decisions that would shape the rest of her life. My visit hadn't changed anything. It hadn't helped at all.

I wouldn't understand for decades the full extent of what broke our family. The letter my father received before we left Connecticut was the beginning. Mr. Hitchcock had been president of the Metropolitan Church since 1925 and wielded absolute power. Gloria—my "hallelujah! amen!" sister—and Glady had followed God's strictly orchestrated plan and gone into church work after graduating from the church's Bible School—the high school—in Waukesha. Muriel attended the Bible School her senior year of high school, too, but my father soon began receiving reports that she wasn't measuring up.

She was pretty with wavy brown hair like my mother's, and even though she wore it pinned up according to the rules, she found subtle ways to style it that twisted the hair code.

Much worse, she liked boys, and they liked her. Mr. Hitchcock wrote a long letter to my father expressing his grave concern that Muriel's behavior might endanger her future in God's plan.

That letter was the catalyst. It triggered my father's decision to sell the farm and move to the Bible School in Waukesha, leaving Muriel without a home after graduation.

At the time, I didn't know that when Glady sent us our Christmas dolls, she had already written to our grandparents in Connecticut, begging them to help her escape from the church.

Though my grandparents had been loyal to the church all their lives, they sent her the money to return to Connecticut. That destroyed my father's trust in them forever. I lost not only a sister but my grandparents too.

The young man who had helped my father wire our old farmhouse was waiting for Glady.

On June 3, 1947, Glady married Elbert Watrous in Quakertown, Connecticut.

Later that year, when Muriel was begging for help, my grandparents did not intervene. That placed Glady in an impossible position, one that would ultimately shatter her relationship with our parents. When she knocked on our door that spring Sunday afternoon, she and Elbert had come to get Muriel, but she wasn't there. Glady encountered my father instead. On Glady's second trip, she succeeded, and Muriel left with her.

The complexity of the situation, the hidden motives, and the withheld truths would only begin to reveal themselves when I was navigating an eerily similar situation years later.

Chapter 7
Camp Meeting

In August, the men of the church were busy setting up large tents for the annual camp meeting on the green lawns across the street from the Waukesha Bible School. The children's tent was across from the steps of the main entrance. Across the street was the big tent for revival meetings. It had two tall center poles like a circus tent and more poles around the edges. The ground was covered with a thick layer of straw, and on either side of a main aisle were about two hundred chairs.

Electric lights were strung from pole to pole, and there was a stage with a piano and room for an orchestra. In the middle of the stage stood the pulpit with an altar railing surrounding the entire area.

The big dining room was also opened. It was used only at camp meetings. It was cavernous with its ceiling murals of peacocks and clouds, faded now but still grand enough to take my breath away.

My mother had been sewing new matching dresses for Linda and me. This year's dresses had red and yellow flowers, and in the middle of the front was a circle of dimity and lace. I loved my fancy dresses, but my shoes were a problem. My feet grew fast, and each time my mother traced my feet on paper to give to the women's buyer for the church, she bought me brown shoes with shoelaces. I was disappointed enough to stamp my feet more than once in my new shoes.

For that camp meeting, new dresses were not enough. All the little girls had shiny black patent leather shoes, and one girl had a pair that were not only shiny but had a strap around the ankles and black bows on the toes. I begged my father for shoes like that. Somehow, he found the money and bought me the shoes I wanted. I walked on clouds and sat with my legs stretched straight out in front of me to admire them.

That night, when I was taking them off, one of the bows was missing. I think my father felt as badly as I did when he told me I'd have to wear them anyway. I cried and tried not to look at the shoe with the missing bow after that.

Everyone in the church came to camp meeting. It was the yearly vacation for all church workers. Families came from the missions and Sunday schools in Fort Dodge, St. Louis, South Bend, Cincinnati, Chicago, and Milwaukee, as well as California and Pennsylvania. The grand dining room was opened, and all the rooms and dorms were filled.

I discovered quickly that Glady and Muriel were not there. "Where are they?" I pestered my mother.

Finally, she answered, "I guess they wanted to get married."

Linda and I joined about forty children in the smaller tent every morning. We listened to Bible stories, which were new to me. We hadn't attended Sunday school or church in Connecticut. My mother was busy taking care of her sick parents, and with gas rationing during the war, my father couldn't afford to drive to Providence, Rhode Island, the nearest Metropolitan Church.

When Linda and I returned to our rooms each morning after our meeting, we carried on an argument that teetered on blows. We learned a new chorus each day and always told our mother that the other one was singing it wrong. One morning, my mother listened to Linda and went to the piano. She could play by ear, and when I recognized the music, I chimed in with the words.

"You are a perfect team," my mother said. "Linda learns the tune and you learn the words."

That was okay with me. Not every argument ends with both parties being right.

Mrs. Sammis was in charge of the children's meetings. She was saved and sanctified but didn't have any children of her own. We sang, "Jesus loves the little children, all the children of the world." We sang "The B-I-B-L-E, yes, that's the book for me" and learned John 3:16: "For God so loved the world."

When Mrs. Sammis asked, "Who wants to give their heart to Jesus?" my hand was the first to shoot up. Bursting with big emotions, I placed my hand in hers, and we left the tent and walked across the street. We climbed the steps to the grand entrance with the tower above and entered the Bible School lobby. The walls were lit with polished sconces. The wide planks of the floor were covered with a rug woven in such an intricate pattern that I tiptoed across it. There was a large cage in the back, the reception area from when it had been a hotel.

We walked down the hall and stopped at a closed door. Inside, the room was empty except for rows of chairs. When we knelt, I put my elbows on my chair. Mrs. Sammis closed her eyes, and I closed mine. I repeated the words after her. When she said amen, I said amen.

"Now you are saved!" she said, hugging me. Then we walked back to our meeting. "Be sure to tell your mother!" she added.

I did tell my mother, but if I expected her to rejoice, she simply asked who prayed with me. It would be a year before I learned that in my church, we had to get saved all over again if we committed a sin. When I realized what sins were, I began to say the "forgive me for my sins" prayer every night before I slept.

At night, all the children were allowed into the big tent for the first part of the service— prayers and special music. Everyone knelt in the straw, and some prayed out loud. My mother always prayed silently. Linda and I made little golden nests in the sweet-smelling straw. We squirmed as the sharp ends poked our bare legs as we waited for the leader to say amen so everyone could sit in their chairs.

My mother had a beautiful soprano voice and often sang in church services. My heart would beat fast and my breaths were shallow during her solos. It might have been because she charged me with keeping Linda quiet, but watching my mother alone next to the piano, microphone in hand, evoked big emotions. The whole tent would hush, awaiting the first note, and when she sang, her voice filled the night air. I felt she was singing to me, but I always gave a nervous sigh when she finished.

I loved the magical moments when mothers and children filed out after the special music, not because our meeting time was over but because it had become dark while we were in the tent. Our procession cut a swath through the blackness as we whispered or talked in tiny voices on the way back to our rooms.

Chapter 8
Holy Jumper

Linda and I were growing fast, and my mother had to ask Miss Seeley, the church's buyer, for winter clothes for us. I already knew I didn't like Miss Seeley. She was a tiny lady with gray hair in a bun. All the women wore their hair in buns at the back of their necks, including my mother, but Miss Seeley pulled her thin hair tightly back from her forehead. I never spoke to her, but I was sure she didn't like children.

She bought our winter underwear, long-sleeved yellowish-white shirts, and knee-length panties that we called "snuggies." I needed a new snowsuit, and when my mother called me into the bedroom to try on the one Miss Seeley had picked out, any hope I had of looking like the other children at school collapsed. I had dreamed of a little red coat with pretty buttons and leggings with a strap that slipped under my shoes. Instead, she had gotten me a brown snowsuit, not a warm or rich brown, but a dull, monotonous brown, like the floor, like my shoes, like dirt. The jacket and hood had a narrow green line of trim, but I hated it all.

"I won't wear that. It looks like a boy's snowsuit!" I cried.

My tears didn't help.

I was wearing my brown snowsuit the day I learned how the world really saw us. It was a cold winter day, and the snow was deep. At recess, I found a sheltered spot beneath the pines that bordered the public school playground. I was searching for pine cones in the snow when I looked up and saw a big boy, probably a second grader, walking toward me. He wore a plaid jacket and earmuffs. His hands were in his pockets.

As he came closer, I didn't know whether to run or stay where I was.

"I know who you are," he said, his cheeks squashed into a sneer.

"No, you don't," I said, staring back.

"Yes, I do. Everyone knows you're a holy jumper."

"I am not! You don't even know me!" But I was already talking to his back.

Little doubts about what he said grew bigger as the afternoon wore on. When I got back to our family's rooms, I called to my mother. With a hint of desperation in my voice, I asked, "Mama, am I a holy jumper? A boy called me a holy jumper. I'm not, am I?"

"No, of course not," she said quickly, trying to reassure me.

"Then why did he call me that? He said everybody knows I'm a holy jumper."

"They used to call the people in the Bible School 'holy jumpers,' but there are no jumpers now."

"There used to be?" My chin quivered. "Why?"

"A long time ago, people jumped during church when they were happy," she said gently.

I swallowed hard. "Are you sure we aren't holy jumpers now?" I asked.

Her reassurance held until I asked my father that night.

"Well," he said, "when I was a little boy, there were some pretty good jumpers." He got a faraway look in his eyes. "My Uncle John was the best jumper in the Bible School. At camp meeting, he would run up the aisle, jump over the altar, and do a handstand in front of the pulpit."

That was all I needed to hear. My uncle was a jumper. I really was a holy jumper. How could I not have known?

One afternoon after lunch, I trudged back to school through the snow. One moment I was kicking dirty slush, and the next I was staring at something that stopped me in my tracks. It

shimmered and swirled, an explosion of rainbow colors dancing in the frigid air. I scrambled over the snowbank piled along the curb and squatted beside a big puddle for a closer look. The day was overcast, but a few beams of sunlight broke through, sparkling on the surface of the water.

Pinks and purples, reds and greens melted together and spread out, shifting shapes faster than I could follow. Iridescent blues and turquoise danced and twirled across the surface. I held my breath. It was the most beautiful thing I had ever seen. If everyone could see it, I thought, the world would be a happy place. There would be no people calling me a holy jumper—and no ugly snowsuits. Everything would glisten and gleam. It would be like heaven.

When I looked around, I realized the playground was empty. The bell had rung, and I hadn't heard it. If I went in now, everyone would see me, the little holy jumper sneaking into the back of the room to take off her ugly brown snowsuit.

So I turned and walked slowly back toward the big old building where I lived. I would make trails and build a snowman until I saw the other children going home.

When I entered our family's rooms later that afternoon, my mother looked at my rosy cheeks and the sweaty ginger hair plastered to my forehead under my hood. My mittens and snow pants were soaked.

"Why did you play hooky?" she asked, her voice laced with concern.

I told her about my beautiful, wonderful, astonishing discovery, something I would never forget.

She said it was an oil leak from a car and that I had better not skip school again.

Chapter 9
Linda

Linda reached up to catch the twirling red and yellow leaves that the wind twisted from the trees as we kicked and shuffled our way home from school. I was in third grade and she was in first. We waited for each other outside the school doors, and I always checked to make sure she had her sweater or coat and that her kerchief was tied under her chin. Cold air was bad for Linda. She had already been sick and missed school that fall.

We were almost home, and I was still searching for the perfect leaf for our mother when I glanced up. A big white truck was parked in front of the Bible School near the side door that we used. Grand Avenue was one of the widest streets in Waukesha, but the truck should have been facing the other way.

I took Linda's hand, and we began to walk faster. Almost running, I pulled her across the street. Both of the front doors on the truck were open, and as we approached, I saw someone inside.

"What are you doing here?" I said with a dash of confidence. "We live here."

The woman in the white truck wore a white jacket and stood in front of a large black box. She smiled down into my upturned face. My rosy complexion and freckled nose were a sharp contrast to the pale little girl trying to peer around me. Linda's kerchief was sliding down from her red hair, and her face was as white as a ghost.

"We've been taking X-rays to check for tuberculosis," the woman told us. "I'm all done for the day."

"But we live here," I repeated. "We need an X-ray."

"Well, okay," she agreed. She wasn't looking at me; her eyes were on Linda. We waited until Linda could catch her breath. The woman wrote down our names and then took our X-rays.

"Your mother will be hearing from us soon," she said.

"I know about X-rays," I told Linda as we pulled open the heavy doors of the Bible School. "They have them in shoe stores. You put your foot in, and you can see your bones." I don't know where I got that idea. I'd never been in a shoe store, but I was confident the pictures would show our bones.

My mother didn't seem thrilled when I told her about the X-rays. But every afternoon after school I asked, "Did the pictures come yet?" Every day she told me no until the day that changed our lives forever. When I asked about the X-rays that afternoon, I knew something was wrong.

Mother sat down. "Today I got a letter about the X-rays," she said.

I had a bad feeling. Whatever I'd done getting those pictures was turning out terribly wrong. I held my breath. Linda was waiting too. My mother told us that Linda had a problem with her heart. Something did not close properly; she had a hole in her heart. Linda began to cry.

I knew Linda got sick easily. Her legs ached. Her ears ached. Her lips turned blue if she ran. But we didn't know she had a hole in her heart.

"Did you know about this before the X-ray?" I finally asked.

"Yes," my mother said. "Linda was born like this. But the X-ray showed her heart is working so hard that it has gotten larger."

So now, not only did Linda have a hole in her heart, but her heart was beating so fast that it might wear out. Maybe my mother chose that moment to tell us because I had been so persistent. But it unleashed a flood of questions that never ended.

Why was I healthy and Linda was not?

Why did Linda have a hole in her heart?

What if Linda died?

Linda looked at me through her tears. I was so sorry—sorry that we had found out, sorry that she had to know she could die while she was still just a little girl. In the days that followed, my mother tried to explain that God had a plan for everything and that Linda's heart was part of His plan.

I was confused. I was sad. I was afraid.

If God answered prayers, shouldn't we pray for Him to fix the hole in Linda's heart? My mother said we should pray that Linda wouldn't get sick.

But we prayed for the hole to be fixed.

We still had a lot to learn about where babies came from, but one thing continued to upset me. When God made baby Linda, why didn't He fix her heart before He sent her down from heaven? That was a terrible mistake. I had to believe it was a mistake. God knew about it, and He just let Linda be born anyway. Understanding that life is not fair is hard for anyone. I was seven.

Chapter 10
Heaven and Hell

In the days that followed, Linda and I talked about making sure she would go to heaven if she died. We knew all about heaven. Good people went there when they died. We knew about the streets of gold and the pearly white gates, about the angels that flew around and played music.

We even had a special one called a guardian angel. This angel could keep us from getting hit by a car or falling off a mountain. But only God decided when we would die.

We also knew about hell. There was the Judgment Book where God made a list of who was bad and who was good. Sinning would knock you right off the good list. But we couldn't stop sinning every day. Saying a mean word, being slow to obey our mother, tattling, hitting, or telling a lie—they happened every day.

We spent time wondering which kinds of deaths would give us the longest moment to say "I'm sorry." We never doubted God would forgive us. But the problem was having time to ask.

One night we were kneeling beside Linda's bed where we always prayed since she was often sick. Our prayers went on and on as we asked God to bless every member of our family and anyone else who came to mind. We always ended with "forgive me for my sins" and the little prayer:

> Now I lay me down to sleep,
> I pray the Lord my soul to keep,
> If I should die before I 'wake,
> I pray the Lord my soul to take.
> For Jesus's sake, Amen.

As I finished, Linda began to cry. Her sobs turned to hiccups. My mother heard her panic.

"I'm afraid I'll die. I don't want to die."

We never said that little prayer again.

When winter came, Linda stayed home from school. My mother taught her, and I carried her schoolwork back and forth to her teacher.

One afternoon I came home and saw a small clipping from the newspaper on the table. Most of the words were too difficult to read, but it was about a doctor and a heart and an eight- year-old girl.

"Mama!" I burst into the bedroom where my mother sat at the sewing machine. Linda was at the little red table. "Did you see this? Read it to me!" She looked up. When she saw what I held, her face told me it was something I wasn't meant to find.

"Please," I begged. "It's about a doctor who fixed a little girl's heart!"

Linda jumped up and tried to grab the paper from my hand. My mother sighed and took it. She read aloud:

> Dr. Robert E. Gross of Boston, MA, has achieved a groundbreaking medical feat with the first-ever successful patent ductus operation.....The first successful

> operation was performed on an 8-year-old girl named Lorraine Sweeney on August 26, 1938.....This procedure brings hope to countless families.

"Mama," I said, jumping up and down, "that doctor can fix Linda! He fixed that little girl. Please, are you going to take Linda to have her heart fixed?"

Linda's eyes sparkled. She reached for the paper again.

"Can we get Linda's heart fixed?" I begged.

"It costs money," my mother said, her voice soft and sad. "And it's new. Not all the little children live after they get this operation."

I wilted where I stood. Linda would not give the paper back. The sparkle had left her face, but I found one more ray of hope.

One day I was reviewing the Ten Commandments for Sunday school and said to her, "Linda, listen to this." 'Honor thy father and thy mother, that thy days may be long upon the land which the LORD thy God giveth thee'" (Exod. 20:12).

"Linda, this is what the Bible says. It means if we obey our parents and do everything they say, you will live a long time."

Now we had a way for her to live. We tried. We really did try.

Chapter 11
The Rumbling

That spring, I was eight years old. I had never been to a store. I rode in a car once a year. I had begun to hate going into the Bible School when other children walked by on the street to go to their homes. I heard them talk about "doing dishes" and wished I could do that too. I was beginning to feel the rumbling of "different."

My pigtails had grown longer, and standing still while my mother combed my fine hair was a daily chore. Then the other two little girls who also lived in the Bible School got their hair cut.

"We want a haircut too!" Linda and I begged and pleaded.

My mother said something that left me stunned. "Your father wants you to grow your hair long now. That's what women should do. It says so in the Bible."

The rumbling storm inside me crashed down. All the women in the Bible School wore their hair long, twisted, braided, or rolled. Was I to become one of them?

"No!" I shouted.

"It's what your father wants," she said.

This was the first time I connected my father to the church rules. But it would not be the last.

My sister Gloria, the next oldest, embraced the church, rules and all. She followed Mr. Hitchcock's yearly mission and canvassing appointments as though they were the voice of God. That year, she was back at the Bible School in Waukesha working with the high school girls. About six of them had won a contest, and their prize was a trip to Pewaukee Lake, Wisconsin. Gloria said Mr. Hitchcock had a cottage there, and I could go with them.

It was a rainy weekend at the cottage. I stood alone, looking out over the lake. A small semi-circle of windows extended over the water, and I felt like I was in a rocking boat. Raindrops dashed against the panes, and gray waves rippled and bowed. A sudden rush of emotion took my breath away. I wanted to live here in this little house on the lake. The water was close enough to touch. Our huge old building felt far away and ugly.

Gloria had said this was Mr. Hitchcock's cottage. I had lived in the church commune long enough to believe that what was mine was yours, and what was yours was mine (except for my mother's furniture). But now, a flood of feelings passed through me. This cottage was his. It was not mine. It was not ours. And it never would be.

School was almost out for the summer when I was invited to a birthday party for a girl named Janet. Once again, I pleaded with my mother. I don't know if I brought a gift, but I turned up at the doorstep. That afternoon was a whirlwind of questions in my soul. I saw little girls in party dresses I couldn't have imagined. Pink crepe paper streamers and balloons decorated the room. I watched Janet's mother walk into the kitchen, and I inched toward the open door. There was the white stove where she had baked the birthday cake—and then I saw it: a round cake with white icing, pink flowers, and candles.

I had never seen a little girl's birthday cake.

I walked home in a daze. The truth struck: I did not live like other girls, and I never would.

Chapter 12
Leaving

The day after school let out, my mother awakened us while it was still dark. We slurped our cereal with our eyes half closed. "What are we doing?"

"No questions now," she said. "We are going away."

Linda and I followed closely behind her toward the garage where the church cars were kept. My father was talking to the garage man. I saw Gloria and her friend, Alice Knowles. Gloria had our little black Christmas dog, Cookie, on a leash.

Why was Cookie here? Gloria handed me the leash and told me to walk around. Linda followed me. The sky was beginning to lighten over the Bible School, and we shivered with excitement in its soft, warm glow. I circled back around, bewildered, questions piling up.

It was obvious that wherever we were going, Cookie was going with us. My mother was calling us over to a car—no, not just a car but also the attached little silver travel trailer. I tried to run back to get a better look, but our mother told us to get into the car. I sat in the back between Gloria and Alice. Linda was in the front between our parents. My mother had placed a little cardboard box with a blanket near my feet for Cookie.

When my father started to drive, I couldn't hold back any longer.

"Where are we going?"

"Wait a little longer and I'll tell you all about it when Daddy gets out on the highway," Mother said.

This was big. There was daylight enough to see expressions. Gloria looked like she knew what was happening. Alice stared out the window. I could see the side of my father's face—his lips were tight, almost scowling. I couldn't read my mother's face. Linda was squashed down, and I knew she couldn't see out the window. I tried to look behind us.

"Why are we taking that trailer?" I asked.

This time my mother began to talk.

"I will explain to you," she said. "We are leaving the Bible School."

"Is this a vacation?"

"No," she said. "We are not going back."

"Are we going to Connecticut?"

For a moment, hope flared that I might see my grandparents and sisters again.

"No, we are going to live in the trailer."

"Forever?"

"No, just for now," she said.

Gloria began telling the Bible story about the Israelites leaving Egypt. I had no idea what she was talking about. "God is leading us into the Promised Land," she said, her voice alight with excitement.

Later that morning, we stopped beside the road to let Cookie out. I stepped into the empty field, and my heart soared. I looked up at the blue sky—as far as I could see, there were no houses, no big buildings. We were never going back to the Bible School. I looked down at the blue cornflowers and white clover and wanted to shout. I had seen many flowers, but these would stay in my memory forever. I didn't care where we were going. All I needed to know was that we were not going back.

We drove into the afternoon. I sat by the open window with the wind blasting in my face. Linda was still squashed in the front seat. My mother was fanning her, brushing sweaty hair from her forehead.

"Marinette," my father said. "We're going to find a trailer park in Marinette." Later I would learn this was a city on Lake Michigan, about 200 miles north of Waukesha.

Gloria and Alice rented a room over the laundry-shower building in the trailer park. Linda and I discovered our tiny bedroom at one end of the trailer. Our parents would sleep at the other end.

That evening after supper at our little table in our little kitchen in the trailer, Gloria sang in her sweet, high voice as she washed the dishes:

> Be not dismayed whate'er betide,
> God will take care of you.

Cookie sniffed around and lay down under the table.

"Mama," I called from our little bedroom, "Will you stay in the trailer with us all night? Will you still be here in the morning?"

When the sun rose the next morning, we were all in our little trailer. I began to put the Bible School away forever.

Chapter 13
Trailer Park

"Where is Floydie?"

That was the first question of the first day of our new life. My fifteen-year-old brother was in Denver for the summer with Mr. Hitchcock, his wife, and some of the church members.

The trailer was not big enough for all of us. That was the easy answer.

A second question came right on its heels: "Why did we leave the Bible School?"

We had left the Bible School with plans to never return, and the reason was not so easy to understand.

"Some of the men on the church board voted Mr. Hitchcock out," my mother explained. I wasn't sure I understood what a church board was, but I knew how important Mr. Hitchcock was. For twenty-five years, he had been God's voice, relaying God's messages to the church, ordering everyone's life, selecting missionaries, choosing and ordaining preachers, and assigning canvassers who went door to door selling literature to make money for the church. He was also the one who would not let people get married.

"Since Mr. Hitchcock can't run the Bible School anymore, we have to start a new church," my mother said.

That made perfect sense to my eight-year-old brain. I had lived in the Bible School during four critical years of childhood development. My worldview was limited, and my parents were right. If we were going to heaven, we needed Mr. Hitchcock.

To make sure, I asked one more question: "Are all the people who voted against Mr. Hitchcock going to hell?"

My mother's answer was vague, but heaven got smaller when just one hundred people in our new church were going there.

"Everything will work out," my mother reassured us. She quoted Romans 8:28: "And we know that all things work together for good to them that love God, to them who are the called according to His purpose."

Because it was summer and our questions were answered, Linda and I tumbled out of the trailer to explore. We turned away from the busy highway and walked to the end of the trailer park, staying clear of the other trailers. New houses were being built beyond the park, and three towering piles of dirt marked our stopping point.

We were looking beyond them, however, for just on the other side was a little girl about our size. We stared at her, and she stared back.

"Shall we ask her to play with us?" I asked Linda. She didn't answer.

"She looks dirty," I said, trying to make up my mind.

"I guess we could ask her to go home and take a bath and put on a clean dress so we can play," I finally decided.

The little girl nodded to my request and ran toward a house down the street. "I think we made a new friend," I told my mother when we returned to the trailer for lunch.

That afternoon, we walked back to the end of the trailer park, and our friend was waiting. She was wearing a clean dress. We played in the dirt piles all afternoon. That night, we wore little rubber shoes and learned how to take a shower in the washroom of the trailer park. In the morning, my mother made breakfast for my father, Gloria, and Alice while Linda slept and I lay awake.

I smelled toast and listened to the clatter of dishes and silverware. Then a pause—my father began to read the Bible. They began to pray as they knelt around the table. My mother's prayers were sweet. My father's were long. Gloria's were awesome. Her voice rose higher and higher with each request until she was talking straight into heaven. By the time she got to her "Amen," she was singing like the angels. I knew it would be a good day whenever it was Gloria's turn to pray.

Then my father, Gloria, and Alice went canvassing. They sold books and cards to earn money for the new church.

At supper one night, Gloria's high voice signaled excitement. "We are going to the Fourth of July fireworks!" she said. Gloria was twenty-three, but that night we were little sisters together. She tried to give me a lesson on Independence Day, but I was too excited, dancing and prancing among the crowds. We stopped along the grassy banks of Lake Michigan, a cool breeze coming off the water. I sat on a blanket between Gloria and Alice. As the sun set behind us, there was a hush, and then a sudden boom bounced me up and down, my pigtails flopping.

The first fireworks shot into the night sky, bursting into brilliant red and blue spiraling patterns. Everyone cheered and clapped, and Gloria shrieked with them. I looked up at her and braced for the next explosion. It shook the night air, spreading like a magical golden flower into the sky. Soon Linda began crying, and we picked up our blanket. Gloria pulled me along, but I planted my feet. I turned to watch the twinkling pink sparkles fizzle into the choppy water of the lake.

Through the years, Gloria would be the fireworks of my life, her brand of religious zeal tugging at my soul.

Shortly after the Fourth of July, my father hitched up the trailer, and we moved again. After a long drive, we settled in a grassy corner away from the other trailers in a small trailer park. A tree provided shade, and my father bought rope and put up a swing for us. He prayed happy prayers and embraced each day. My mother was more subdued. We saw her reading her Bible where she kept four-leaf clovers pressed between the pages.

On Sundays there was no canvassing and no church service, so we spent our time walking along the country roads with our father. He taught us the difference between milk cows and beef cattle. We could recognize what was growing in the fields. "Knee high by the Fourth of July" was how to measure the height of corn stalks. Before the purple flowers appeared on the alfalfa was the time to make hay. The fields of winter wheat were changing color, and our father told us the threshing machines would arrive when the fields were golden brown. We learned the names of the grasses growing beside the road, and every Sunday when we walked, a blade of timothy was hanging from our teeth as we chewed the sweet, tender end.

One Sunday, my father was silent. He did not answer our questions or seem to notice that we trailed behind him. We stopped on the bridge over the White River and stared at the fast-flowing water as it carved a path along the muddy banks. Linda and I picked up pebbles and threw them into the water, but my father continued to gaze beyond the curve of the river into the trees.

I would not learn until later that my mother had upset the equilibrium of our family and jarred my father's commitment to Mr. Hitchcock. She had put her foot down and given him a check on reality.

"This trailer belongs to the Bible School," she told him, "and only God knows what Floydie is doing in Denver. It is past time to get him back into the family. Do you think Linda can survive the winter in this tiny trailer?" She bore down. "We won't be able to stay warm, and what will we do when Linda gets sick?"

Not only that, but she pointed out that the shower room was a good distance from the trailer, and we'd have icicles hanging off us after a shower. We'd have to take baths in a galvanized tub again unless my father acted.

Chapter 14
The House

Owning private property was not God's will, according to Mr. Hitchcock. To get into heaven, we must give up all. According to the Bible, God's people were to have "all things common" (Acts 2:44). My father had sold the farm in Connecticut for Mr. Hitchcock, and now my mother wanted him to buy a house again, this time in Wisconsin.

By this time, Gloria was breathing fire as she searched for a place to start a church high school. God's plan to grow the church was not to raise Christian families—although in my father's case, an exception had been made. The church needed canvassers—unmarried canvassers. That was what my sister Muriel had been doing in Cincinnati—selling things door- to-door to spread the Word and get money for the church. The new church needed a high school to educate young people to follow God's will and become canvassers. Students were recruited from the Sunday schools the canvassers established.

Gloria found a retreat in Lake Geneva, Wisconsin, and the call went out to the canvassers for money. By late September, the high school opened at Lake Geneva with ten students, my brother Floydie among them.

My father did not take my mother to see the house he found in the village of Union Grove, Wisconsin, just a thirty-minute drive from Lake Geneva. He purchased it for $5,000 with a $1 down payment and a mortgage of $50 a month.

At the beginning of August, he hitched up the trailer for the last time and parked it in the driveway of the house—an old white farmhouse with a kitchen and bathroom addition hanging off the back. The street was paved when we turned into it, but it became a dirt lane as we caught our first glimpse of our new house. In one direction, we were a block from the railroad tracks; in the other direction were the town dumps.

"This is home!" my mother exclaimed. Her smile lit up her face as we bounced out of the car and raced into the house. The floor sagged and creaked as we scuffed across the peeling linoleum of the large dining room. I heard my mother ask my father to open the windows to air the place out. My father obliged, but most of the windows had been painted shut. Not a second after he managed to force open one sash, it crashed down with a bang that made my mother shudder. A huge, black, pot-bellied stove with silver handles squatted between the stairs and an open doorway. "This is the dining room," mother said, and through the open door to the parlor was another pot-bellied stove.

My mother stood looking at the stoves, her forehead wrinkled. "Is this all we have to heat the house?" she asked my father.

"There's another little stove in the kitchen to heat the water," my father answered. He looked at her as if waiting for approval. "I'll get in a supply of wood," he said. "The stoves are big enough to keep the place warm."

Linda and I found the kitchen at the end of the dining room and took a moment to balance ourselves on the sloping floor. Our parents followed closely behind, my mother exclaiming, "This kitchen is wonderful!" She ran her hand along the white stove, turned on the water at the sink, and opened the door of the Frigidaire.

While we were exploring, my father slipped out the front door and drove away, leaving the trailer behind. A few hours later, he returned with a truck and a man from the church in the cab with him. We stood speechless, our eyes as big as saucers as they unloaded my mother's furniture—her maple bed, her mattress, the dressers, and the blue chair. They had even brought the piano and the couch we'd had at the Bible School in Waukesha. I had been certain we would never see that furniture again, but I knew even then how much it meant to my mother.

My father and Mr. Goode, the church man, left with the truck for the Salvation Army to get more furniture. Meanwhile, my mother began opening the cardboard boxes that had been unloaded from the truck after the furniture. We had brought them from Connecticut and stored them at the Bible School. She held up a plate with a double gold band around the rim. The box was full of dishes with gold trim. She wrapped the plate again and placed it gently back inside. "This was a wedding gift from Aunt Nora and Uncle Em," she said, her eyes bright.

I didn't remember my relatives in Connecticut well, but the boxes sent shivers of excitement up my spine as my mother unpacked items from her life before Bible School. They must have come from the old house we used to live in.

"This is a cedar chest," she said, lifting the lid of a long wooden box. "This was my hope chest from Daddy when we got engaged. I hemmed sheets and made blankets to put into it.

I decided I would get a hope chest someday. I admired the sheets—no longer new— tablecloths, and quilts, and tucked the memory away in my wedding dreams. We had Army blankets at the Bible School, but these quilts were made from old woolen men's suits, big squares of black and brown with occasional navy blue. They were lined with thick padding and tied with string knots.

We examined a special quilt my mother's friends made before she got married. Some quilt blocks were smooth, shiny cloth; some were soft velvet. Her friends had met together to make the quilt, and each of them had made a block and embroidered my mother's name and a special message on it. The idea sounded sweet, and I made a mental note to add a friendship quilt to my wedding wish list, along with the cedar chest and gold-rimmed dishes.

When my father and Mr. Goode returned, they unloaded a huge wooden box I could stand in—a wardrobe, my mother said. "Put the wardrobe in the girls' room," she directed, and my ears immediately perked up. At the Bible School, we slept in the room with our parents, but I stood beside my mother and watched as the men set up a heavy black double bed and mattress in a smaller room off the parlor. It was our bed in our room. This was turning into heaven.

Mother scraped her fingernails over the mattress and pressed her hand into the creases. "Just making sure there are no bedbugs," she said. "It's a bit stained, but that's no problem."

Our room had one window and three doors. Besides the one that led out into the parlor, another opened to the backyard. But when it swung open, I saw there were no steps, and the door was several feet off the ground. There was a hill, and it was too far to jump. I opened another door that went from the bedroom to the cellar. It was dark down there, and the steps looked steep. When the door was open, a musty smell crept into the room. I decided not to open those doors again.

We didn't know that Union Grove was only 30 miles from Waukesha. To Linda and me, we were hundreds of miles from the old Bible School.

Chapter 15
Canvassers

My father had gotten Mr. Hitchcock's approval to buy the house. Canvassers were coming to live with us, and my father would drive and canvass with them. My mother would be the housekeeper. Soon, canvassers Dorothy, Betty, and Ida moved into the room under the eaves upstairs. By the time school started in September, everything was going according to God's plan. Linda and I went to public school and then played under the horse chestnut trees in our yard, collecting smooth, shiny brown conkers from pointy green husks. We picked bunches of goldenrod and wild purple asters for my mother on our way home from school. The parlor became our parents' bedroom so my father could tend the stoves. Our room was only a wall away from them and the stove.

But as fall slipped into winter, the temperature began to drop. I was wearing shoes I had outgrown, and my old brown snowsuit was two sizes too small. But I was now going to school with children who lived on farms or in apartments over the stores. They dressed as I did, and we lived in a house that made me feel rich.

What did matter, however, was staying warm. My mother would dress me in my snowsuit and hood with a scarf tied around my face, leaving just enough room for my eyes. I sometimes trudged to school like a stuffed sausage, only to have the janitor tell me school was canceled because of the cold. A radio would have helped, but it was against our religion.

Once it got cold, Linda didn't go to school. When I got home every day, I played with her near the stove to stay warm. But the house kept getting colder, and conversations at the dinner table carried a note of worry. My mother had been right about the old pot-bellied stoves. They belched smoke, and the damper on the black stove was stuck. The only wood my father could buy was green and wet, and it gave off little heat. The ladies upstairs—the canvassers—froze at night, despite the hole that had been cut through the floor above the parlor stove. They said a cold wind blew in from the north window, and they shivered all night, even under woolen quilts. Two weeks later, they moved and went to a warmer house in Chicago an hour and a half away.

But before they left, my father always drove us to the high school in Lake Geneva for Friday night church services. One Friday afternoon, it started to snow as I walked home from school. My mother offered a gentle warning to my father at supper. But nothing could keep him from God's people, and soon I was in the back of the car, wrapped in a wool quilt, listening to the crunch of snow under the tires. My mother and Linda stayed home. I stared out the windshield as the wipers struggled against the caking snow. White ice arrows flew into the glass, and my father's gloved hands gripped the wheel. The chatter of the three women turned into prayers.

I whispered with them, "Dear Jesus, please take care of us."

The preacher at the high school was Leon Graham, the church's vice president. Leon was second only to Mr. Hitchcock, who had picked five members for the school board. My father was one of them. Everyone was already kneeling when we arrived, and I knelt at the only vacant chair on the women's side, the front seat right in front of the pulpit, close enough to feel the preacher's breath. The room felt steamy after the frigid car, and when the preaching started, I began to itch. One itch after another kept me squirming and biting my fingernails.

When I looked up, Leon Graham was glaring at me. For a moment, I worried he would call out my name. But he wasn't my father or my teacher at school, and I hoped he didn't know who I was. Shriveling under his stare, I held my breath, folded my hands in my lap, and tucked my feet under the metal chair. When I peeked up again, he looked away, but shame hung over me.

I turned nine in November. Our family's life revolved around going to church. We went at least twice on Sunday, on Wednesday night, and on Friday night. My mother often stayed home with Linda. Even after the three canvassing ladies left for Chicago, nothing stopped my father and me from showing up to every single service of our church.

The temperature kept dropping until we woke up to zero or below almost every morning. My father was getting up in the night to coax the weak flames. He was awake more than he was asleep. Finally, in desperation, he walked across the tracks to the Farmer's Co-Op and asked for some corncobs to keep the fire burning. They gave him a gunny sack of corncobs. They also told him they needed another truck driver since the bitter cold had increased the demand for coal. My father took the job.

Chapter 16
Stop!

Linda and I played together every waking hour. We argued as sisters do and at times could sound like the worst of enemies. I was sure by this point that our father was tired of raising children. He had already done the fun things—sledding and snowball fights—with my three older sisters and Floydie. By the time Linda and I came along, he was over it all. We just got on his nerves.

One day at the table, Linda and I wouldn't stop bickering. The argument was insignificant, but we were both stubborn and determined to have the last word. Our mother asked us to settle down, and for a while, we did. But something started us up again.

Suddenly, my father reached out and slapped my face. Red Jell-O flew out of my mouth and onto the floor. I jumped up and ran to my room. I was too shocked to cry. I had never seen my father like that, but of course, I had never talked at the table when we were at the Bible School.

A few days later, Linda and I launched into a new, equally petty disagreement. We were nagging at each other the way kids do when our father grabbed us both by the backs of our dresses and pushed us into our room. As he made us bend over the bed, he took off his belt. A raw snapping sound broke through our protests, and Linda inhaled sharply. Then she began to wail. The next smack of the belt landed on the backs of my legs. Blow after blow fell onto our soft skin as he moved back and forth, alternating his strokes while we screamed. We begged him to stop. We cried and shouted desperate apologies.

Finally, he stopped. He stood there for a moment as we gasped for air. Then he silently left the room. I helped Linda up onto the bed. We whimpered and rubbed our eyes and noses. Her legs were covered with swollen red welts, and even her back had crisscrossed stripes. When our mother came into the room, I jumped up and grabbed her hand.

"Look!" I cried. "Look at Linda's legs." I had marks on my legs, but they were not swollen like Linda's.

"Why?" I gasped, confused, angry, and afraid. "Why did Daddy do that?"

My mother stood still. The silence felt heavy after the chaos of the previous moments. When she finally spoke, her voice was sad. "I guess it's the way his father punished him," she said. After that day, I watched my father carefully. He had never touched us at the Bible School, but maybe we hadn't fought so much there. Now, he was quieter than ever, and when he prayed, his voice cracked. His eyes would not land on me or Linda.

In spite of my father's actions, my mother's Christmas spirit refused to be contained. We had our Christmas tree with bubble lights and tiny glittering angels. Since money was scarce, there weren't many presents, but on Christmas morning I found a gift from Gloria: a pair of ice skates from the Salvation Army. They were like the ones I had outgrown—boy's black hockey skates—but at least now I could skate again. And I did, every night after school at the pond by the dumps until it was dark.

I learned our family's holiday traditions that year. Gloria and Floydie were home, and on Christmas Eve my mother made oyster stew. Linda and I each had one wrinkled little blob hiding in a bowl of warm milk. My father smacked his lips, and my mother beamed. I was more excited by the dish of mixed nuts and the nutcracker.

On Christmas morning, my father arranged apples, oranges, grapes, and bananas in a glass bowl, a tradition carried over from the time when a single piece of fruit was a rare treasure.

I could hear Gloria's high-pitched voice in the kitchen as she and my mother prepared the New England version of a holiday meal. We had turnips mashed with the potatoes. There were boiled onions floating in milk and butter, and for dessert, there was mincemeat pie. As I ate the sweet pie, I crunched on the dried fruit and tried to taste the ground meat I knew my mother had added. I didn't ask for seconds. Maybe I wasn't as much of a Yankee as I thought.

When I had a chance to find Gloria alone, I asked her a question that had been bothering me. "Why isn't Daddy on the church board anymore?" I had overheard talk and wondered if that was why our father seemed so sad.

"I guess it's because he bought the house and took that job," she answered. "Mr. Hitchcock didn't approve." She didn't tell me the job had lasted only the month of December. But now my father had a house to pay for, no canvassers, and no place on the board.

Chapter 17
Night Vigil

The sun was shining in my eyes, making me squint at the white, feathery patterns of frost on the inside of my window. Linda was still sleeping beside me in the big double bed when our father walked through our room and down to the cellar, carrying the empty coal scuttle.

I climbed out of bed and followed him down the narrow cellar stairs. My mother told me he brought home a load of coal yesterday. His truck driving job had been temporary, but after Christmas, the Farmers Co-Op gave him a permanent position. The dank, damp smell of earth hit me, and then a freezing blast of air smacked my face. I stepped barefoot onto the cold, packed dirt floor. Sunlight struggled through a small rectangular window at ground level, but shadows lingered. My father set down the scuttle and reached for the coal shovel. That's when I saw a pile of coal cascading from the rafters in the corner.

"How did you get the coal down here?" I shouted above the grind and clatter of coal sliding into the scuttle.

My father jumped and turned around. "I backed up the dump truck and used a chute through that little window," he nodded. There was another small window, the same size as the other one hiding above the coal. No light was coming through, but I remembered that thick shrubs grew there just outside. A little invisible window—I liked that. But it was cold. My father sent me back upstairs, and I was happy to crawl into bed again. As he clomped up the stairs, I saw his old black work boots with hooks for the laces. He closed the cellar door, and I saw the frayed cuffs of his blue work shirt and his striped overalls. I liked having a daddy with a job. Life was good, I thought. Life was just as it should be—our little family in our own house and my father bringing home the money.

The next afternoon, as I walked home from school past the Farmer's Co-Op, I thought about the coal. Where was it? Instead of crossing the railroad tracks, I turned and walked alongside the building. There were four cement bins next to the railroad tracks filled with black piles of coal sloping down like a hill. One was filled with little chunks of shiny black coal. I saw dull gray coal, and the last bin had smooth little pockets of coal that rose all the way to the train tracks. This was like the coal in our cellar. I knew if I followed the tracks, I would come to a field just below our house. So I climbed the coal pile that day and walked along the tracks. Climbing the coal became my favorite way home from school until the pile got too low for me to reach the tracks.

Then I played another game as I walked home. I imagined a black Model A Ford slowly following me. An old man was driving, and his wife sat beside him, smiling and pointing at me. When I reached our driveway at the bottom of the hill, I glanced back. Grandma and Grandpa weren't there. The Model A wasn't there. But I would keep playing my game. Someday they would come.

All winter, my mother taught Linda at home, and I stopped at the second grade classroom to return her work and pick up new assignments. Linda was coughing, and she wasn't sleeping in the double bed anymore. My mother had set up a cot for her beside the big black stove in our parents' room. When I came home from school one afternoon, Linda lay propped up in my mother's maple bed. I dumped a stack of books on the bed for her. I had discovered the town library sandwiched between the drugstore and a brick building with the sign "Knights of Columbus" above its double doors. In the back of the library was a long table with black chairs where the town meetings were held. On the lowest shelves were the picture books that Linda liked; a shelf above were the stories I loved. I discovered the Laura Ingalls Wilder books, and the librarian ordered the rest of the series for me. But Linda didn't want the books I brought home that day. She pushed them onto the floor. She was really sick.

That night, my mother read *Heidi* because Linda loved the part where Clara got out of her wheelchair. But tonight, Linda closed her eyes, and my mother stopped reading.

"Go into the bedroom," she said to me softly, closing the book. "Let Linda sleep."

I learned a lot from my parents' prayers during morning devotions at the breakfast table. There was thanksgiving for my father's job, but when Linda became sick, my mother's prayers changed. She was not just asking God; she was begging Him. We didn't have a doctor yet, and Ellen, the Bible School nurse, was far away. Our house smelled of Vicks VapoRub that my mother slathered on Linda's chest and covered with a warm rag to help her breathe.

There was no reading the next night, and as I knelt to say my prayers, I whispered, "Mama, is Linda going to be okay?"

"We are praying for God to touch her," my mother said. "Dorie, you pray too. God answers prayer."

I fell asleep listening to Linda's rasping cough.

When I came home from school the next afternoon, Gloria and her coworker Alice were there from Lake Geneva. I peeked into the room where Linda lay, her eyes closed, her little chest rising and falling as she struggled to breathe. Her heart was pumping so hard that the sheet covering her moved up and down.

My mother wasn't at the supper table. She was sitting beside Linda's bed as we silently ate. Afterward, Gloria surprised me. "Put on your snowsuit," she said. "You and Alice are going to the drugstore."

It was a clear night, and moonlight guided us as we threaded our way through the ruts in the snow. Our breaths puffed out in white clouds. A light bulb illuminated the sign above the Clover Farm Grocery Store where my father drove my mother every Friday night for groceries. Next was the town tavern. Across the street, I could see Schwartz Hardware where Billy Schwartz and his family lived upstairs.

The drugstore was warm as I followed Alice inside. "Would you like to get something at the soda fountain?" she asked.

"Over there?" My voice was a pitch higher than a whisper as I pointed toward the row of red stools along the counter. She nodded, and I scampered toward the counter before she could change her mind. I'd seen my classmates drinking soda and eating ice cream there last summer, and I knew exactly what I wanted.

"I would like a lime phosphate." I reached for the shiny glass of neon green soda, pulling it closer. I sucked through a paper straw for the first time. My drink was exactly what I had imagined, tingling my tongue with its sour-sweet tang. I glanced back, wishing my classmates could see me, but only Alice was there. I pushed my straw into the ice cubes at the bottom of my glass and listened to the gurgle and hiss of the last drops.

I didn't fully grasp until much later that the night of my great adventure in the drugstore was the night Linda was fighting for her life while my family desperately prayed.

In the morning, I tiptoed past Linda's cot beside the stove. I could see her chest rise and fall. No one was with her. The floor creaked as I walked into the kitchen. "Did Jesus touch her?" I asked my mother. The worried lines were gone from her face.

"Yes," she nodded.

I could see God's hand extending down with lightning bolts from His finger as it rested on my sister. My mother and I breathed happy sighs.

Before the next winter, Mr. Goode helped my father install a furnace in the cellar.

Chapter 18
Easter

The snow was melting, and in school we were singing "In Your Easter Bonnet."

Linda and I were seven and nine and getting new Easter dresses. We sat at the dining room table, sorting through the brightly printed cloth feed sacks my father had brought home from the grain elevator. My mother had washed and ironed them and stacked them in neat piles. White string looped around the edges.

"Make sure you pick from the feed sack piles where there are at least four alike," my mother said.

One stack had sacks of gray, yellow, and white stripes; another had tiny boots and shoes in purple and orange. I lingered over the blue teardrops with red dots that my mother called paisley, but I chose the white background with big purple flowers and little blue daisies. Linda wanted the pink checks with blue bows, even though our mother said red hair and pink didn't go together.

Our new church had purchased a little white chapel on Lanham Street in Milwaukee, about a half hour north of Union Grove. After months of long drives to Chicago each Sunday, we had a shorter drive now and could go to Sunday school before the long sermon. A group of women canvassers brought children whose parents let them come to Sunday school if they were picked up and dropped off. The Sunday school girls had short hair and curls. The teachers smiled at them warmly as they walked in. “So glad you could come,” they said.

Maybe today the teachers will see me, I thought, smoothing my new purple-and-white Easter dress. When the other children walked in, my heart dropped to the bottom of my brown shoes, which I had polished the night before until they shone.

Most of the girls were strutting in dresses with ruffles and lace. They were the dresses I always dreamed of with thin, shiny cloth and underskirts that poofed out. One girl had a little suit with a dark skirt and a white checkered jacket. They had Easter bonnets too.

“I hate that Sunday school,” I said as we drove home.

“Shut your mouth!” my father roared.

My mother looked back at me, her eyes pleading. I repeated to myself, *I hate that Sunday school*, even with the little bag of blue and pink Easter eggs in my lap. The candy was too sweet and hard.

“Complaining will get you nowhere,” my mother whispered softly before turning her head toward the front.

Chapter 19
Floydie

After Easter, my brother was sent home from the church school at Lake Geneva. He was a senior, and I never knew what trouble he was in, but he did not go back. He moved into the tiny room in our house at the top of the stairs. It had no heat, but my mother gave him two heavy wool quilts. There was just enough space for his bed tucked under the sloping roof and a closet with a door so short you had to crawl into it. He was sixteen and soon graduated in June from the public high school in Union Grove.

One Sunday afternoon, Floydie and I hiked through the field below the dumps and into the woods. He climbed the barbed-wire fence, steadied himself with his hand on the fence post, and jumped. I could do that too, but when I jumped, my dress with purple flowers caught on the barbs, and the back of the skirt ripped to shreds.

"Stop!" I wailed, tears beginning to roll down my cheeks.

My brother looked back. "Go home if you want," he shrugged. "I'm going to find pussy willows." I wiped my eyes, but with each step, those little tails of cloth tickled my legs, and the tears in my eyes threatened to slip down my face.

We found bushes of pussy willows beside the wide creek that ran through the farmer's land. Little gray buds dotted the branches, and I petted them, smooth and soft like the fur of my cat, Tippy.

"Mama will be excited," my brother said, glancing back at me as I trudged behind him. "She loves pussy willows."

I knew what he was not saying. She would not love the back of my dress. Our mother was excited about the pussy willows. She put them in her green Depression glass vase.

Then it was my turn. I turned around. Linda gasped. "It was the fence," my voice choked. "I have enough feed sacks to make a new back panel for your dress," my mother said. I looked at my brother and wrinkled my nose.

That bunch of pussy willows was later moved to the high chiffonier in our bedroom. It was still there when Linda and I would not stop arguing. My father grabbed the pussy willows and began swatting our bare legs. Big angry red welts appeared on Linda's skinny legs. He stopped abruptly. I looked up and bit back my scream. My brother was at the door, glaring at my father. Little gray balls of pussy willows dotted the floor. I tried to pick them up, but my tears were in the way.

We got chickens that spring and kept them in the garage. They were not fluffy yellow baby chicks but already had short white feathers. "Pullets," my mother called them. "They'll be laying eggs by the end of summer." Then one day a truck pulled into the driveway. We heard squealing, and I ran over to the truck and peered over the tailgate. Linda could not see into the back of the truck, so I counted: "One, two, three, four little pink and black pigs," I told her. "Wait, there's another one. It's so little that the other pigs are on top of it."

"It's the runt," my father said, coming up behind us. In almost the same breath, he added, "These pigs are farm animals; you can't name them."

The runt became Pinkie, but we didn't tell our father.

Linda and I were walking home from school on a warm spring day, a thin gray veil of mist dampening our faces. "April showers bring May flowers," I chanted. "Tomorrow is the first of May." I had not yet found the spot in the woods where white-spotted dogtooth violets grew, or the pond on the farmer's land where wild purple iris waited to be discovered.

But on May first, my brother drove us to the florist. We went down the road toward the sauerkraut factory. In summer, the smell of rotten cabbage gave our town its distinctive aroma. We parked in front of a little store and followed my brother into "heaven." There were buckets of flowers in every color and size. I saw red roses and yellow and white as well. I recognized carnations and daisies, but everywhere I looked, there were new flowers I had never seen. I touched my nose to the roses, their sweetness perfuming the whole room. As the lady folded the flowers in newspaper, she told my brother she was adding free baby's breath. I ran over in time to see white clouds of tiny flowers like delicate lace around the flowers.

Linda and I knew the May basket story, and my brother was turning it into a magical dream. He made a little basket, filled it with flowers, and hung it on our front door. Then he knocked, and we all ran around the side of the house and waited. My mother had tears in her eyes when she opened the door and saw the basket of flowers.

On another May Day in Connecticut in 1924, my father had driven up in his family's Cadillac and hung a May basket on my mother's kitchen door.

"Some fella is here to see you," one of her brothers had called out.

My father's family was well known in Quakertown, Connecticut. These once farmers had moved from Quakertown to Chicago when my father was just a baby to join the Holy Jumper Church there. They had since returned, and my father had met my mother and brought her a May basket. My mother ate the chocolates from her May basket that spring day in 1924 and immediately fell in love. That was how the Quakertown girl met the Holy Jumper man.

The flowers from the florist that Floydie and I gave our mother remained in the green Depression glass vase until all that was left was a heap of faded petals on the table.

That summer, my mother began to complain about flies. "Those pigs are too close to the house," she told my father. One day the pigs were gone, and my father was nailing screen wire to the frame for the kitchen door. My mother gave him a spool from her thread box for the handle of the new screen door.

"Something is getting those chickens," my father announced one day. The chickens had left the garage and were wandering in the backyard. We could hear their whirring clucks as they scampered away from us. There was a rooster, too, and I would wake up early in the morning to his cock-a-doodle-doo.

The next day I saw a little skinned carcass hanging from the branch of a tree. "I got that possum," my father said. After that, we began to eat the chickens for dinner, but not before we ate the possum. "Not bad," my father said, scooping up a bite of possum stew.

I watched my father grab a chicken by its legs, lay it over a stump, and with one swing of the axe cut off its head. "You should see it when he lets it go," my brother said, watching. The headless chicken jumped off the tree stump and started running around. I ran to the house screaming.

Steam was rising from a bucket of boiling water next to the kitchen door. My father arrived with a headless chicken that he held by the feet and dipped it into the bucket of boiling water. He plucked off handfuls of wet feathers and handed the carcass to my mother.

After that, the chicken became my mother's work. She singed it, holding it by its legs over the fire on the little kitchen stove. An acrid smell stung my nose as the downy feathers burned off. I gagged and turned away. "Watch me now," my mother said as she pulled out the stubby little white pinfeathers on the wings.

"There are three things you have to know," she told me. "You already know how to darn a sock, and you will learn how to iron a man's white shirt. But pay attention because every girl has to know how to clean a chicken." This chicken was becoming an important education. I learned fast, slitting the gizzard and cleaning out the grassy mess. I cut the little green gall bladder off of the liver. My brother told me liver was the best part of the fried chicken, and I agreed. He always ate the drumsticks.

My brother's birthday was in August. He was seventeen and had a job at the Ford dealership at the top of our street. My father was in his garden when he wasn't at work, and my mother was making me new dresses out of feed sacks for school. She was also filling the shelves in the cellar with jars of canned tomatoes and green beans. My father had built the shelves in the cellar next to the stairs.

Early in the morning, I would go down to the garden. Ever since my father let me pull the first radishes and bring bright, curly green leaves of lettuce up to the house, I went down to help him before he went to work. One day he reached into a row of feathery green leaves and pulled out a perfect long, orange carrot. He wiped it on his overalls and handed it to me. The juicy sweetness mixed with the crunchy dirt as I chewed. I carried the first red ripe tomatoes to my mother and learned to feel the ears of corn to know when they were ready to pick.

Inside the house, it was not always peaceful. Linda and I argued, and sometimes there were blows. "She started it," I claimed, defying my father's order to stop.

"No, she did," Linda would get the last word.

One whipping followed another, and it was always Linda's legs that showed the worst red welts. When she cried, her breath came in great gulps, her heart visibly thumping under her dress.

I stomped out of the bedroom after one of our whippings and heard raised voices outside. My father and brother were beside the lilac bush, their faces close together, although my brother was 2 inches taller than my father. "Get out!" my father roared. "You think you can tell me what to do? You're leaving." I had heard those words before and now it was my brother.

It was very quiet in our house that night. My father took my brother to the train station and bought him a one-way ticket to Connecticut. After that, my father never whipped Linda again. He ordered me to the cellar and used a belt. Years later, my brother told me he had threatened our father if he ever whipped Linda again.

After my brother went away, I walked down to the bottom of the garden where the pigpen had been. My brother had scratched our names—Linda and Dorie—in the dirt and planted sweet alyssum seeds in the grooves. The tiny white and lavender flowers were blooming, all jumbled together.

"Goodbye, Floydie," I whispered.

That winter Great Aunt Jessie came to stay with us. She was my grandmother's sister and had been a missionary with the Metropolitan Church in India. My parents moved with Linda to the large room upstairs now that we had heat from the furnace. I moved into Floydie's old room at the head of the stairs so Aunt Jessie could have my bedroom with the door to the cellar. My new room had no heat at all. All winter, I wore a flannel nightcap, had a hot water bottle on my toes, and burrowed into thick layers of woolen quilts. In the morning, the frost on the inside of the window was so thick that it took all morning for it to melt off.

Aunt Jessie introduced me to a pen pal named Shirine Patrick in India. We wrote to each other, and in her letters she told me she was meeting with the boy she would marry when she was eighteen. I told Aunt Jessie I couldn't write to someone who didn't know or follow church rules. I knew you had to leave the church if you got married, like my sisters Glady and Muriel had done. I wanted to stay with my mother and father in the church and go to heaven. Why had Aunt Jessie given me a pen pal like that?

Chapter 20
The Visit

The summer when I was twelve, we all took a day trip to Potomac, Illinois, to see the new school buildings our church had purchased. We drove 200 miles directly south from Union Grove, Wisconsin, through Chicago, and past mile after mile of Illinois farmland.

I didn't yet know about my sister Gloria's brilliant plan. She was aiming to accomplish two things at once: increase the enrollment of our Christian school, which had only eight students, and save me from another year in the evil world. She was proposing to add eighth grade to the high school so I could attend.

We drove into the town of Potomac, population 602, and my mother reached into her purse for the scrap of paper with directions. "Turn here," she said, pointing. We were on a narrow cement-slab road, just wide enough for one car, with dirt shoulders for passing. "Now we're looking for a road on the left," she added. Four miles down the road, we found the dirt road. "Close your windows," my father said, one hand on the steering wheel and the other cranking his window. Clouds of dust billowed around us. Before we could get them shut, I could already feel the grit on my teeth.

"Oh my," Mother said. "This is really in the boondocks."

We turned again onto another dirt road. Then we saw it—a three-story red brick building rising out of the cornfields. My father turned onto the driveway between two stone pillars. We passed the brick building and stopped beside a slightly smaller gray building across from a farmyard and barn. Chickens ran loose, and an old orange tractor was parked nearby. Linda and I jumped out of the car. My father walked toward the barn, but my mother called us all back.

"We are guests here," she warned. "Stay with me." We entered the gray building together, only to find more gray inside. The linoleum on the floor was buckled, and wallpaper strips hung from the walls. Near the door, mounted on the wall, was a brown wooden box with a crank on the side.

"Stop playing with the phone!" my mother snapped as we spun the crank. Who knew a phone didn't have to look like the little black one on our table at home? Our ring was one long and two shorts on our four-family party line. I glanced back at the wall-mounted contraption and wondered if it rang like ours.

We were in the kitchen, which was recognizable only by a huge black iron cook stove in the corner and a dirty sink. In a room off the kitchen stood a white refrigerator that covered an entire wall. All its doors hung open. My mother called to us from a little hallway on the other side of the kitchen. "Look," she said excitedly. All we saw were cabinets and shelves with a sink under a small window.

"In rich houses, this is called the butler's pantry," she said.

Linda and I found the stairs. At the top was a long hallway with smooth brown linoleum stretching the length. There was a window at either end. This would become the girls' dormitory. We opened doors along the hall. Each room was the same with peeling, faded paint on the walls, wood-planked floors, a window, a closet, and a rusty radiator. One room was a small bathroom with a tub, sink, and toilet. There was a shaving mug and a wooden-handled brush like the one our father used.

"Somebody must live up here!" We ran downstairs.

After inspecting the barn, my father joined us, and we walked together to the three-story brick building. It was built entirely of brick and cement. In the early 1930s, a philanthropist had built it as a school for young women, but it had been empty for twenty years. In the spring, our church bulletin had included the first news of the property. God had provided it, and all the canvassers worked extra hours to pay for it.

Linda and I led the way, running up the wide cement stairs into the brick school building. Two sets of double doors opened into a large lobby. A wooden bench under the only window welcomed us. The space was dark and cool even with the bright summer sun. Two large schoolrooms occupied the first floor. One had a wooden stage about a foot high. Blackboards with peeling paint lined the walls, and above one, a stone slab was engraved with "God Is Love."

"I'm getting a good feeling about this place," my mother said, gazing up at the stone plaque.

The other room had a similar slab: "The Truth Will Make You Free." My mother got her good feeling again.

We explored two more large rooms on the second floor. The third floor had many small rooms that would become the boys' dormitory.

Linda and I followed our father into the basement. There were two more large rooms. We found Ray Goode there. He had helped our father install our furnace at home. He was working in a dark little room on the boiler and furnace, which would provide steam heat for both buildings.

Later that afternoon, on the way home, my mother turned and looked at me. "Would you like to go to that school?" she asked.

"I guess," I answered. "I'm not a fan of dirty windows and cracked paint. Maybe they will fix it up by next year."

"No, I mean this fall," she said. "They say it will be ready by September."

"Lots of work," my father said. "We'll see."

I leaned close to Linda. "Do you think Mama will let me skip eighth grade?"

Linda didn't answer.

By August, the church had purchased an industrial-sized stove for the kitchen. The refrigeration worked, the furnace and boiler were repaired, and the electricity had been inspected and approved. There was a new telephone, and the number was printed in the weekly church bulletin. All that remained was painting and cleaning, and several church women had been recruited.

Gloria's plan was coming true. And the new school would have eighth grade.

Chapter 21
Summer Days

That fall, I was a student at this church school, and I was in the eighth grade. Annie was the other eighth grader. In Waukesha when I was four, she and I had sat on the grass for a photo in front of the children's camp meeting tent. Her family had lived down the street from the Waukesha Bible School, and three of her siblings had gone to high school there. One of her sisters had joined the church after graduating from high school. Annie and I had seen each other only once a year, at the church convention. She was pretty and taller than I was. She had white-blonde pigtails.

She had just visited me in Union Grove that summer. One night before we crawled into bed, I opened the door of my room—the door with no steps outside that dropped off down the hill. We looked out at the sky, brilliant with stars.

"A shooting star!" I cried.

"Another one!" Annie shouted. Another, and another, and another.

Later, I learned the Perseid meteor shower came every year in August. We would remind each other of those magical moments and remain friends throughout the years. But summer wasn't over yet. One afternoon, I sat at the bottom of the hill with my back against a tree. The swing nearby stirred in the breeze. My notebook was open on my lap, my pencil in hand. I loved the story I was writing, pausing over the names and ages of my twelve children. I erased the five- year-old boy's name and changed it to Allen. Satisfied, I continued. I was describing the house for my big family when Gloria came up behind me.

I jumped, snapping the notebook shut.

"May I read it?" she asked. I handed it to her, watching her face. She wouldn't like it. I'd written about getting married and having children. I was pouring out my dreams, and I knew my dreams weren't God's plan.

No one had explained the doctrine to me, but at twelve, I understood. Mr. Hitchcock had long ago made the rule: Members couldn't marry because they had to canvass and make money for the church. Gloria was praying for me to follow the Lord like she had and become a canvasser, but I was already dreaming of marrying, like Glady and Muriel.

Even if I left the church, I was worried. I wasn't pretty or popular like the girls with boyfriends. I had more than a smattering of freckles across my nose and cat-green eyes, and I was chubby compared to Linda.

Gloria finished reading and handed me back my notebook.

"Do you like it?" My eyes were pleading.

"Well," she said, drawing out the word, "keep on writing. You'll improve."

Maybe my writing would improve or maybe the content of my story? She never asked to see my writing again.

I was done writing for the day, but I sat thinking after she left. Besides the problem of the church and my freckles and chubbiness, there was another terrible fact: Boys asked girls out. I'd received only one Valentine that year, and it was from the boy nobody liked. I had one idea. I had heard that every four years, on leap year, February 29, a girl could ask the boy. I'd need to start planning now to get it right.

It was twilight at the end of a long summer day. My father came around the house from the garden. I was standing in the driveway, listening to lively music drifting down from the park in town. It was Family Night at the movies. What could be wrong with that?

"I want to go," I called to my father. "I really want to go to the movies."

"No!" His voice boomed loud enough to still the crickets.

Silence hung in the air. Then I turned and sprinted up the road. Gravel crunched behind me. My father caught the back of my dress and spun me around. His arm connected with my face. Blood spurted from my nose. He grabbed my shoulder and shoved me through the front door, the dining room, and my bedroom, all the way to the cellar door.

It was predictable. He had tried to whip the rebellion out of me too many times to count. He chased me down the steps. Leaning forward, blood dripped from my face. There was a pause as he reached for the belt. But it took too long. I turned. He wasn't holding his belt. His arms were raised, gripping a 2"x4" wooden plank.

"He's going to kill me!" I screamed, bolting up the stairs and out of the cellar in search of my mother. I buried my face in her dress, clinging to her waist. She pried me loose, helped clean my face, soaked the blood on my dress in cold water, and sent me to bed.

The next week, my father bought a secondhand blue girl's bicycle. I had begged and prayed for a bike like that for three years. I practiced riding up the hill and down the farmer's lane. I was almost getting the hang of it when I had to leave it behind.

Chapter 22
Convention

It was Sunday, the final day and final meeting of the church annual convention in Lake Geneva. I was swinging my Bible, merging with the stream of people on the path to the auditorium. Linda was running along beside me. Tomorrow would be the most exciting day of my life. Tomorrow I was going to the church school for eighth grade at the new church school in Potomac, Illinois. I saw my parents waiting for us beside the auditorium.

"Dorie," my mother called. "We want to talk to you." She nodded toward the block wall at the back of the building. "Linda, wait here."

My heart sank. This must be bad news. They were going to tell me I couldn't go to the church school tomorrow. Angry words piled up on the tip of my tongue. I would argue so loudly that everyone would hear me. We stopped at the wall, and my parents turned to face me.

My mother spoke again. "Dorie, Daddy wants to say something."

I silently screamed. All the fight in my adrenaline system flooded my veins. I looked him straight in the eyes. I was already a sick mess from a week ago.

"I want to say I'm sorry," my father said, his voice low. "Will you forgive me?"

I deflated and took a step back. "Of course." I stared back and forth between my parents' faces. I would forgive anything if I could go tomorrow.

"Let's find Linda," my mother said, and we mingled with the people going up the stairs to the meeting.

The heat of the August afternoon blasted my face, and the sounds of swishing skirts and muffled footsteps exaggerated the stillness of the holy place. Windows were open along both sides of the room, and fans in the ceiling rotated slowly. I was numb from my father's apology as I followed my mother and sister into a middle row of folding chairs on the women's side. I could see my father make his way into one of the three rows on the men's side. There would be empty seats around him, but on the women's side every seat in ten rows would be filled. All of the canvassers came for convention.

I sat down. My breathing slowly returned to normal, and my shoulders relaxed. My brain wanted to rip into what had just occurred, but it was a sore too fresh to pick.

I concentrated on the backs of the women filling the seats in front of me. Hours in church services with the same view enabled me to recognize most of them. There were far more pairs of black old-lady shoes shuffling past than brown oxfords worn by the younger women. The predominant hairstyle was a tightly coiled bun resting on the back of the neck. Curved tops of tortoise hairpins stuck out around the edges of gray hair. The younger women wore their hair in braided loops. I raised my hand to the back of my head, poking at the wire hairpins holding my braids and adjusting one that stabbed into my scalp. My bangs were growing out. Women in our church did not wear bangs. The sides of my head above my ears were plastered with bobby pins to hold my bangs back.

Sitting in the middle of all these women, my brain raced. They were old maids, just like our card game, my mind mocked. I squeezed my hands and clamped my jaws at the terrible thought. What if I ended up like them? Thoughts crowded in. They would never get married. Mr. Hitchcock let Leon Graham get married the first year after we left the Bible School, but in the years that followed, there were no more weddings. These single people supported the entire church, including the missionaries, and of course, Mr. Hitchcock. But important to me, the canvassers had provided the money to purchase the buildings in Potomac where I would go to school. These were the people who were giving me the opportunity to attend that church school.

An anticipatory intake of breath hung in the air as Mr. Hitchcock rose from his seat and stepped behind the pulpit. The love and adoration flowing out toward him could only be eclipsed by their love for God Himself. Our leader's thin, wrinkled hands trembled as he opened his Bible. I had no idea how old Mr. Hitchcock was. He might have been sixty, seventy, or eighty, but when his voice projected across the room, I could see everyone eagerly awaiting his every word.

My mother nudged me. Her Bible was open, and I had not heard the text. Glancing over, I opened to Romans, chapter 8. Mr. Hitchcock began to read: "But if we hope for that we see not, then do we with patience wait for it" (Rom. 8:25). How much patience did I have? Just how long was I willing to wait? My family was full of rebels—Glady, Muriel, Floydie. It was only a matter of time for me. Internally, I was already rebelling.

A black hole filled the space where my heart should have been when I caught a glimpse of my father across the room. He sat straight in his starched white shirt, staring intently at Mr. Hitchcock, focusing on the words to save his soul. His prayers and tears were witness to his struggles, but I knew he fought a losing battle. Was it my fault for keeping his salvation out of reach?

I told him I forgave him. Did my mother make him apologize? It felt strange to forgive my father, but maybe he was really sorry.

Mr. Hitchcock closed his Bible, and collectively, all the Bibles in the room flipped shut. When the pianist struck the introductory notes of the closing hymn, I knew every verse by heart. Tears rolled down the faces of the women around me, and my mother's voice resonated on the last two verses:

> Blest be the tie that binds our hearts in Christian love;
> The fellowship of kindred minds Is like to that above.
> When we are called to part, it gives us inward pain;
> But we shall still be joined in heart, and hope to meet again.

My emotions snagged in the sad hugs and farewells of canvassing crews preparing to leave for another year of service. I slipped outside. The sun had disappeared, and thunder rumbled in the distance. The first big raindrops bounced off my nose. I paused before turning back. I was breathing the breath of freedom, and my cocoon was splitting.

Tomorrow my parents and I would make the three-and-a-half-hour drive to Potomac, Illinois, and I would emerge into a brand-new life. The odor of perspiring bodies hit me as I stepped inside again, but I was grounded in tomorrow, and my spirit soared.

Chapter 23
Eighth Grade

The next day, my father and I set my shiny black trunk down in the parlor of the gray building in Potomac. My father returned to the car, and excitement blurred my ache of goodbyes as I waved to my family and watched our blue Ford disappear into the dust of the dirt road. Clutching my little white purse, I ran inside.

The five girls who had attended the church school in Lake Geneva were there, and the contrast for them was stark. In Lake Geneva, they had lived at The Maples, an elegant Maytag mansion near the lake. Now we were in the middle of Illinois farmland in an old 1930s building that had spent its last decades storing grain. The nearest water view was a pasture creek across the road.

The gray building housed the girls and the women staff. The dorm was upstairs where Linda and I had chased each other on our summer visit there. Now the rooms were painted pastel yellow, pink, or blue. Doors, windowsills, and high mopboards gleamed white. Radiators wore silver paint, and white asbestos tubing covered the steam pipes. A roller shade was in each sparkling-clean window.

Patty, my roommate, helped me carry my trunk upstairs. I felt her eyes on my back, and my self-confidence dropped with every step. Our room was at the west end of the hall, the farthest from the barn's sights and smells. The hot summer sun danced on dust motes from the open window. We set my trunk in the middle of the floor. Patty gestured toward the bunk beds with their thin mattresses tucked tightly against the back wall.

Patty was short compared to me. Her dark brown braids were pulled back, with wispy curls framing her round, rosy cheeks. She was a junior, age seventeen. I was twelve.

"Top or bottom?" she asked.

"Top!" I got to choose. Already, I liked Patty and our room.

Patty grabbed her sheets and began making the lower bunk. I knelt on the wooden plank floor and carefully opened my little white purse. It held two one-dollar bills and a tiny flat key for my trunk wedged in the corner. Opening my trunk brought a wave of longing for my mother. We'd packed it for weeks, checking and rechecking the required list I knew by heart. Girls must wear skirts, blouses, and dresses with sleeves and hems below the knees. (Slacks under dresses were allowed in gym class only.) Don't forget that nylons are an everyday attire. A worried frown had creased my mother's forehead at the nylons.

My history with nylons began the previous Easter. In the car coming home from church, I discovered the first run. "Take off your stockings," my mother said as we reached home. "I'll see what I can do." Snags ran up and down both legs; and another run was starting in the toe. The next Sunday, she handed me a new pair of nylons and said, "You just have to be more careful."

By the third Sunday and third collection of runs, she decided socks were more practical for summer. How could parents afford nylons? Gloria had the answer: thick lisle cotton stockings. My mother bought four pairs of heavy brown cotton stockings and packed matching thread to sew up runs. They had a seam up the back and reinforced heel and toe.

As I arranged my things in the two bottom drawers of the chest, the first supper bell rang. Patty turned just as I was frantically throwing overflow items into the corner of the closet. I saw the shadow pass across her face, and then she pointed to two empty closet shelves and hooks along the wall. My cheeks burned.

"That was the first bell," she said, turning away from my mess. "We go down for supper when the second bell rings. You have time to put the rest of your things away."

The dining room had high, white, wooden chair rails and wallpaper patterned with green ivy loops. White linen tablecloths and heavy gray-white plates reminded me of the Waukesha Bible School, and a surprising surge of belonging almost made me smile. I sat with six girls and six older women on the side of the room near the kitchen. The men and boys—three boys and five staff—sat at a long table by the wide parlor door.

After the prayer, bowls began circulating. Each of us had a baked potato, but a bowl of white food moved slowly as girls took tiny spoonfuls. "It's cottage cheese," the school director said as it reached me. I took a large scoop. But it wasn't like the cottage cheese my mother ate. Hers had big, creamy curds. My first bite was sour and grainy. It was made from milk curdled with vinegar, pressed in cheesecloth, and hung to drip over bowls on the kitchen stove. Dessert made up for it—white cake with chocolate sauce called cottage pudding. Lots of "cottage" around here, I thought.

I recognized most of the Bible School staff. Uncle Dan, the gardener, had been married to my grandmother's cousin. Mr. Hubbard, the bent old preacher who officiated at my parents' wedding, read Scripture with a trembling voice. The Freymiller brothers taught school. They were sons of the missionary nurse Ellen who had helped care for Linda at the Bible School.

After supper, Miss Jury, the girls' matron, called the first prayer meeting in the parlor. She wore a bright print dress that matched her big smile. We formed a circle on folding chairs. She explained the schedule, emphasized that we'd be learning etiquette from Emily Post's book, and reminded us to wear deodorant. I felt a surprising rush of belonging as I looked around at all the skirts covering knees, the stockings sagging at the ankles, and braids pinned back. At least in appearance I fit in.

"Lights out at 9:30," Miss Jury said. "The rising bell rings at 5:30 a.m. Be up with smiles for the first day of school."

The big iron bell, bolted to a post outside, clanged at 5:30 a.m. sharp. I threw off my sheet and stepped out of bed.

"First one up," Patty giggled as I crashed down from the top bunk and sprawled on the floor. I trailed close behind her to the basement girls' bathroom. Fluorescent lights over the mirrors left the rest of the room in shadows. The other girls called out good morning as they combed their long hair, braided it, and pinned it up. I was the last one to finish. Patty frowned when I got back to our room. She was already dressed and making her bed.

"We have room inspection after breakfast," she reminded me, smoothing her sheets and batting my sheet hanging over her bunk. She placed her Bible on her bed and plopped onto her knees. "Devotions are for half an hour before the breakfast bell."

I chose my red and blue plaid gingham dress and was still struggling with my stockings, straightening the back seam and fastening the garters when the first bell rang. Patty put her Bible down, gave me a long stare, and then stepped on the edge of her bed and pulled up my sheet. I didn't know if it was help or a strategy to avoid failing inspection. "Thank you," I whispered.

The next morning, I jumped around on my bunk, making my bed before climbing down. I watched Patty as I braided my hair. I turned my back like she did and dressed with newfound speed. When devotion time began, I slumped to my knees. Maybe tomorrow I'd start devotions.

School began with Bible study in the "God Is Love" room. Then my friend Annie and I separated for eighth grade. Our classroom bore the inscription "The Truth Will Make You Free." A stack of worn textbooks waited on our desks. I opened my arithmetic book and saw names scrawled inside.

"Where did these books come from?" I blurted.

"Raise your hand, even if there are only two of you," Alice—now Miss Knowles—said. She'd become strict.

I found out that the books came from a Chicago warehouse full of retired city school textbooks. Chicago books sounded official, and I felt oddly satisfied.

Chapter 24
Work

After the last class, we carried our books to our rooms and changed into work clothes. Miss Jury was waiting at the bottom of the stairs with assignments. Two girls skipped off happily to the kitchen. Two received cards for cleaning bathrooms. They stood there confused until Miss Jury shooed them along. Two got janitor work in the school building.

"And that leaves you," Miss Jury said, turning to me and pointing at thirty tan, metal folding chairs stacked against the wall. "You'll wash the chairs. Get a bucket of soapy water and a rag from the basement." I knew how to clean. She'd be pleased.

When I got back with the bucket and rag, I reached for the first chair. There was a bar connecting the front legs where you could hook your feet. I would give that an extra good scrub. Then I saw it—a hollow channel running the length of each leg on the backside. The front of the legs was smooth, but that little groove in the back was filthy. Dirt particles slid loose when I tipped the chair. I was sure no one had cleaned that groove since I'd squirmed on these same chairs as an eight-year-old in Lake Geneva.

I dragged the chair into better light, twisted my rag, dipped it in soapy water, and scrubbed. Four legs per chair; this would take a week. I twisted, scrubbed, changed water, and got a clean rag halfway through. When Miss Jury returned, I looked up from my knees, still working on chair number seven. I waited for praise. Her eyebrows raised. Her mouth opened. She glanced from the gleaming legs to the murky water and then back to me.

"What *have* you been doing?" she asked, her emphasis sharp on *have*. "You had an entire hour. Why haven't you washed all the chairs?"

I sucked in my breath, startled.

"You get an F for today. Tomorrow I expect every one of those chairs to shine."

I had failed. My lips trembled. I wiped my eyes as I dumped the water down the basement sink.

The next day, swallowing my urge to clean properly, I wiped down the rest of the chairs in record time, ignoring the grime in the cracks. Miss Jury smiled. I earned an A.

A few days later, I stopped Miss Jury in the hall. "Are we allowed to go to the library in Potomac? I need books to read. The last book I read this summer was *Lorna Doone*." I added the name of the book to impress her. I saw the blink of her eyes and knew she was familiar with it, an old English love story. If my mother had seen it, she would have forbidden me to read it.

"Why don't you start at the beginning and read through the Bible?" she suggested. "You will be too busy studying and will have no time for library books."

I began to read the book of Genesis. The old English of the King James Version was familiar, and I knew the meaning of many archaic words. When I was ten years old, I had refused to stand and read a verse of Psalms when the pastor asked me to because it contained the word *loins*. Soon, I was poring over stories in Genesis that made *Lorna Doone* seem like children's literature. Who knew that the builder of Noah's ark got drunk and cursed his son when he discovered him naked?

At Thanksgiving, I went home for the first time. Annie, her brother Ed, and I boarded the train for Chicago. At Union Station, I changed trains for Racine, Wisconsin. When I arrived there and stepped off the platform, I saw my parents and Linda. Hugging them felt like I was shedding a heavy load.

My mother and I celebrated our Thanksgiving birthdays together. I turned thirteen. Linda gave me a plaque she'd copied and colored, edged with Xs and Os in a red frame with gold trim. It read, "I must keep my chin up, my eyes clear, always look ahead, and pray often." —Elizabeth Ann Seton (1774–1821).

Then I unwrapped a big box and gasped. It was sleek, white figure skates. I'd wanted them all my life. But sadly I knew the school creek would never freeze like Wisconsin ice.

The vacation was too short. Tears filled my eyes as I said goodbye. Home and school were now wrestling for first place in my heart.

By the end of eighth grade, my transformation was complete. Proof came in the school newspaper where I solemnly proposed that "I would like the rising bell to ring at 5:00 a.m. instead of 5:30 a.m. The Lord has been helping me get to bed at 9:00 p.m., and I think He would help all the others if He knew they wanted more time with Him in the morning before the new day started. —Doris"

Chapter 25
High School

Summer at home went by fast. Fall arrived, and I was full of hope and excitement as I arrived in Potomac for my first year of high school. I was no longer the youngest student. For the first time, my schoolwork became exciting. I had never dreamed that boring arithmetic could turn into a number puzzle like algebra.

My classmates didn't see it that way. While Annie struggled, I found myself earning 100 percent on every assignment. Soon, excelling in my subjects became the goal of my life. I soared to the top of the honor roll and stayed there throughout high school.

Algebra wasn't the only subject that caught my interest. I was also interested in my thick textbook on ancient history. The nations of the Bible were in the history books. They were the nations God hated such as Babylon and Rome, the people Paul addressed in his letter. I was learning for the first time about the Fertile Crescent and the Great Wall of China. Had my teachers in Union Grove known about this? I was sure it would shock my mother.

Miss Jury, who was teaching Latin, decided to read *Ben-Hur* aloud to us girls one evening a week. Soon, I was begging for more and living for story nights. When the book ended, our routine schedule resumed. I wrote in the school newspaper, "Sometimes I get tired of the schedule being always the same, but since there must be a schedule, I like ours. —Doris"

It was an Indian summer day in late autumn when it all changed. The brisk breeze whipped the sheets and underwear dry on the clothesline before we brought out the last basket of wet clothes. We pinned the load of dark clothes on the lines and began to gather the white sheets that were sailing and flapping against the blue sky. I squinted and batted down the puffy pockets where the wind blew up the folds in the sheets like balloons. We dawdled, running along the clotheslines, feeling the clothes in the hope that one more dry garment could stall the inevitable return to the house.

Four long clotheslines stretched in a swath between the apple orchard and the garden. The last dry, curled leaves from the apple trees swirled in dizzy circles to the ground, and I kicked a smashed late apple and watched the yellowjackets fly up. Beyond the clotheslines was the garden, now full of broken cornstalks like scarecrows and brown tomato vines twisted like messy nests.

After noon dinner, Kathy and I washed the mountain of pots and pans. Girls on kitchen duty baked cookies on Saturday morning, doubling our job. Unlike school days, there was nothing on the schedule for the afternoon. On Saturday afternoons, we caught up on letters home, mended our clothes, practiced music, or hung out in each other's rooms. Miss Jury would drive the carryall 4 miles into Potomac at 2:00 p.m., but unless we needed sanitary napkins, a pad of notebook paper, or hairnets, the general store held little appeal. The three girls doing the dishes in the butler's pantry finished and left. Kathy and I dried the last of the pots and wiped the sweat from our foreheads.

"I want to go outside," I said. If it had been any other girl but Kathy, my wish would have faded into nothing. But Kathy was from a farm in northern Wisconsin. If anyone could feel the pull of the fall day more than I, it was Kathy. I was a freshman, almost fourteen, and Kathy was a junior. But at that moment, we were two little kids staring out the window at the bright blue sky.

"Let's run away," I said.

We didn't plan; we didn't even talk about it. We just took off running up the road. There were no houses or farm buildings for at least a mile in the direction we chose—just us and the whole wide world. A long eroded ditch with a hedge of Osage orange bordered one side of the dirt road, and on the other was corn stubble as far as we could see. We slowed down to catch our breath, laughing at our joke. We had no plan, no food, and no clothes, not even a sweater. We were less than half a mile from the school when we heard a car behind us. We moved over, and Ed Freymiller pulled up beside us in the gray Studebaker.

"Get in." His voice was curt, almost angry. I had never heard him speak in that tone before. We got in, and he turned the car around and took us back. When he stopped the car in front of the gray building, he broke the silence.

"Go to your rooms."

As I closed the car door, my mind went blank. It had never bothered me before that our time outside was strictly controlled by our rigid schedule. With three boys on the campus, it was the duty of our matron to protect us and guarantee that the boys and girls never crossed each other's paths. I was a young teen, self-conscious and shy. They should know that I would have turned around rather than cross paths with a boy.

Finally, I heard the knock on my door and followed Miss Jury down the stairs. Ed Freymiller was sitting on a folding chair near the couch. Miss Jury sat down next to the principal. An empty chair was placed in front of them. I had been "caught," and now I was cornered. Chemical energy shot from my toes to my fingertips. The adrenaline rush left me dizzy, and I groped for my chair. Flight was not an option, but they had never seen my fighting side. I would not look foolish and childish.

"Why did you run away?" "I wanted to."

"Are you sorry?"

For running up the road on a beautiful fall day?

"No."

"Do you want to be in this school?"

"No."

I glared at them. It was a surprise to me that I now did not want to be in the school. How had this turned into the greatest crisis of my life? I stopped answering questions.

The next morning, I found myself with a one-way ticket home. Miss Jury accompanied me to the train station and watched like a hawk to make sure I disappeared up the steps and into the coach of the train. Well, that was it. I went from being a shining star in their crowns to a child of Satan. All it took was half a mile up a dirt road.

Back home in Union Grove, I went from being a celebrity to an outcast. I tried to explain that I didn't mean to run away, but I admitted I had committed the crime. I began to worry about my father. He was not just unhappy; he was angry that I had humiliated him. He had already disowned two of my sisters and my brother. Now, I was afraid that the only thing holding him back from disowning me was my age. My mother's disappointment hung in the air like a weight, pressing me down. Linda was confused, so confused that when she came home from school each day that week, she avoided me. The distance between us grew so wide so quickly that I could hardly bear the loneliness.

That was when I realized that my parents had always intended to send me to church school for high school. That was always the plan. But now I had been expelled, and that door was closed. Still, they couldn't imagine that I would stay home, and I couldn't face what that would mean either. Somehow, going back was the only way to hold on to what little goodwill my father had left. It wasn't a choice. It was survival.

I was sorry. I cried and begged, but nothing happened. One morning later that week, my father opened the front door, and Mr. Hitchcock walked into our house. This was the closest to him I had ever been. He had never come to our house before. He lived in Denver. How did he even know where we lived?

Now I was standing with my father and Mr. Hitchcock in the little room off the dining room, which had a door rather than a hanging curtain. I stared into Mr. Hitchcock's gold-rimmed glasses, his white hair framing the wrinkles on his face.

"Are you sorry for what you have done?" His voice was thin and cracking, and his false teeth wobbled behind his lips.

This time I was so sorry I would have promised anything, but my breathy "yes" seemed to fade into the shadows.

"In the presence of God, will you promise to never act this way again? Not only did you break the rules, but your disrespect for authority is the reason you were sent home."

"Yes, yes. I will never do it again," I said. Tears threatened. He prayed for my soul, and I prayed for forgiveness.

My father took me to the train station, and I was on my way back to school. I should have reclaimed my salvation when I prayed with Mr. Hitchcock, but back at school I felt like a backslider. I was the girl who messed up. How could I ask for grace when everyone seemed convinced I didn't deserve it? During girls' prayer meetings as we knelt in a circle with heads bowed against folding chairs, the others prayed for the baptism of the Holy Spirit. Even Annie prayed to be sanctified. Kathy, who had run away with me, had begged for forgiveness and avoided expulsion. Now she was praying for the baptism of the Holy Ghost too.

Back in the Bible School when I was younger holiness seemed like something only the adults needed, that it came with an age requirement. Children need not apply. Even now I was not ready for holiness. Did the other girls know how good they had to be to stay sanctified?

Sophomore year, Linda was now attending the school—eighth grade. I was disappointed when she was assigned a different roommate, but I had to admit that my religion was safer if we kept our distance. I was amazed as I watched my little sister make friends quickly with all the girls. She learned to play the guitar with Kathy, and with only a few lessons, she was playing the violin. She was the queen of animal lovers. She taught the two school dogs tricks, had a parakeet in her room, and cared for an aquarium full of guppies. In classes, I saw her sleeping more than once, but the teachers did not awaken her. She seemed happy with her name near the bottom of the honor roll.

One winter day, all the students crossed the road, ducked under the electric fence with its warning yellow insulators, and stood around a tall stump in the cow pasture to hear Linda deliver a fiery speech. She was inspired by Frederick Douglass, a slave who had escaped in 1838. Linda was determined that a stump speech should be delivered on a stump and persuaded the teacher to give us an outdoor break so all the students could hear her speech. She wore a black stovepipe hat she had made out of paper. Her speech for the rights of free slaves and the end of slave states would have made our abolitionist ancestors proud. Quakertown, our home in Connecticut, had two hiding stations for the Underground Railroad. The tenets of that extremely religious group stated that they would allow no slavery. Linda was singing with our ancestors that day.

When my junior year arrived, my matron was my very own sister Gloria. We called her Miss Whipple. She had replaced Miss Jury who was called to missionary work in Brownsville, Texas.

Miss Whipple was the same enthusiastic sister I had always known. She called for popcorn parties after study time at night. She awarded the winners of competitions with a sleepover at the Shack, an old chicken coop that was dragged down to the cow pasture for missionary training. We cooked our supper there every Thursday night. We hauled our supplies there through all types of weather, our boots sucking mud and our eyes watching for fresh cow pies. On the night of our prize sleepover on the floor, we kept warm with a little pot-bellied stove and melted snow to wash our dishes.

Gloria took us swimming in the Middle Fork River south of Potomac where our church had bought 10 acres of hilly land for a campground. We wore shirts and gym pants without a skirt in the water because none of us had a swimming suit. The mud along the bank squished up between our toes, and fish nibbled our legs. There was a rundown little cottage where Gloria— Miss Whipple— brought our girls' group for prayer and partying. I loved it. I loved anything that allowed me outside the school property.

The low, rounded hills of the campground dipped down to the flatlands along the river. It was not a proper mountain range by any stretch of the imagination, but Mr. Hitchcock named it Mount Moriah for the mountain on which King Solomon in the Bible built the temple of God. Mount Moriah was consecrated as holy ground for church conventions, an old people's home, and girls' and boys' camps. Three buildings were erected there in about two years by a few dedicated men from our church and paid for with money from the women in the canvassing homes.

The first was a dormitory-style building with an identical layout on the ground level and the basement. At one end was a large room for meetings, and at the other end were a communal kitchen, a dining room, and a bathroom. Along the hallway down the middle were eight small rooms, four on each side.

The top floor was to be the old folks' home. More than half of the people who left the Waukesha Bible School with Mr. Hitchcock were nearing fifty years of age or older with no family to care for them when they could no longer canvass.

The other function of the campground was for church conventions. At the top of the hill was a large building for church assemblies with an industrial kitchen and dining room in the basement. On another hill was the third building, a dormitory.

One Saturday afternoon, Gloria drove half of the girls to the bridge over Bluegrass Creek on one side of the school and the rest of us to the next bridge. She told us to follow the creek back and find each other. It was a warm, sunny day, and ripples sparkled on the water.

"I bet we could drink this water," I remarked.

I had no intention of actually drinking it, but it was so clear that I could see the pebbles and rocks on the bottom of the stream bed. The creek made a sharp bend, and as we ran around the trees that cut into the eroded bank, I stopped in my tracks. A steer was dead in the water, its dark, red, bloated body half-submerged in the shallows. My perception of the future began to take shape that day. The vision stayed with me—a foreboding that my reality could be shattered by what I had not yet seen.

Chapter 26
Senior Year

I was now in my senior year at the our church school. Linda and I went home for Easter church service in the Milwaukee church and Sunday dinner with our mother and father. The church service was uplifting, and the words of the closing hymn kept repeating in my head. I had listened with pride to my mother's voice soaring in the crescendo of the chorus:

"He arose! He arose! Hallelujah! Christ arose!"

As a child, I used to want to crawl under the bench when she sang her solos, but after four years in high school, I had come to love and appreciate her gift.

We passed around the minute steaks and mashed potatoes drizzled with rich brown gravy. No special meal would be complete without my father's favorite salad—crisp lettuce with sliced bananas and a sweet, creamy dressing. As we finished our dessert, savoring the last bites of lemon meringue pie, my mother began to speak.

"We wanted to wait until you were home," she said, "to tell you that Daddy and I are going to work full-time for the church again now that you don't need us as much."

"What?" I interrupted. "What are you talking about?"

"The church needs a married couple to run the old folks' home at Mount Moriah. We'll give you both your own rooms there. We've prayed about it," she added. "Daddy wants to raise chickens again and sell the eggs to help support the church."

I was at a loss for words. It had always been tucked into my consciousness that I would become a church worker and go to a canvassing home after high school. In fact, I was looking forward to it. But now my parents weren't giving me a choice. I would either canvas or, be living in the old folks' home at Mount Moriah.

"What's going to happen to our house here in Union Grove?" Linda asked.

"Leon Graham and his family will move in," my mother answered. "They need a place to live, and Leon will be able to preach in both Milwaukee and Chicago. We wanted you to know so you can pack up all your keepsakes this week."

What? Now my things were keepsakes? But it must be God's will. My parents had prayed about it. As Linda and I did the dishes, I felt like crying. I looked out the window into the backyard where my father had fashioned a teeter-totter for us on an old stump. I was not ready to give it all up.

"Mama," I called, as our little black dog, Cookie, ran into the kitchen. "What are you going to do about Cookie?"

"What about Big Red?" Linda suddenly sounded worried. Big Red was Linda's monstrous orange tomcat.

"Cookie goes with us," my mother said as she stood in the kitchen doorway. "Don't worry. Big Red won't be any trouble here. He's an outdoor cat, and this is his home. I'll ask the Grahams to take care of him."

"Are you going to give our doll buggy to them too?" I asked.

"I think it belongs with children. What do you think?" my mother replied.

I had to agree. I felt my heart grow heavy as I said goodbye to my childhood.

Later, we sat in the parlor on our old couch with the slipcovers my mother had made, I glanced around. There was the square hole cut in the corner of the ceiling to let heat from the old stove rise upstairs before we had a furnace. My mother's piano stood pushed against the unused outside door that led to the porch. The braided rag rug on the floor was where Linda and I had spent countless hours playing with our dolls. My throat got tight again. I wanted home to be home, even if I went to work for the church.

The next day, we were each given a large cardboard box. "I have some old towels if you want to wrap your dolls," my mother offered. Linda and I had prayed for new dolls the Christmas I was ten. On Christmas morning, we rushed out to find our gifts. Gloria's voice was high and shrill as always when she was excited.

"This was my doll when I was little," Gloria announced, "and now I'm giving it to you," I looked at the doll. She had tiny cracks on her face. Her eyes were stuck shut. I had to shake her to open them, and the mechanism in her hollow head rattled so much I was sure she would break. Her hair was a blonde wig my mother had bought and glued on.

"She came from the Salvation Army when I was a little girl," Gloria explained. "We were very poor. I knew you would love my doll." Now I swallowed waves of disappointment. I was special to get Gloria's doll, I told myself, trying to make it stop hurting so badly. Linda's doll had been a hand-me-down, too, a Shirley Temple doll that looked almost new.

I tucked my little blue bonnet pin into my box. It was the one I had tried to give Glady when she left. There was still room for something small. I added my card game of Authors, remembering how beating my brother had been the highlight of my day. I had planned to read all the books on the cards as I got older—especially

The Last of the Mohicans, *Jane Eyre*, and *Silas Marner*—but I learned they were worldly and my cards were as close as I would get to reading them.

Later that week, when my father took us to Gimble's Department Store in Milwaukee to buy my graduation dress, my mood brightened. Linda and I stopped to stare at the window displays, almost losing track of our mother as she headed upstairs to the women's section. She moved dresses along the rack, stopping at a spring green dress with lace, tucks in the bodice, and a belt at the waist.

There were four girls graduating from the Bible School, and we had decided to dress in pastel colors—pink, blue, yellow, and green—my color. It went well with my ginger hair and warm complexion, and it was hard not to feel proud as I looked at myself in the dressing room mirror.

Before spring vacation, the seniors had gone to a portrait studio for senior pictures, and when we returned to school, the packages of black-and-white photographs were waiting. I propped my 8"x10" photo on my dresser and stared at it. I liked my smile. I liked my straight teeth with a little gap between the front two. I was wearing my glasses, and I even liked them.

I carried my picture to Gloria's room. "Don't you think I look really nice?" I asked.

She looked at it for an instant. "It's just you," she said with a little laugh. "That's why you think it's special." I walked back to my room. I guess I wasn't special. I was just me. I would always just be me, nothing to feel proud of. Maybe that was good, I tried to tell myself as the hurt settled deep into my heart. "Pride goeth before destruction" (Prov. 16:18).

The first of May with Gloria, Linda, and me all together meant one thing: May baskets. We made our baskets on Friday after school. Girls all over the farm were picking violets, daffodils, and even breaking off blossoms from the apple trees.

"Miss Whipple, I want to go across the creek to look for bluebells," I begged.

With permission, I ran down the road and across the bridge. I climbed the gate into the pasture. Dodging cow pies as I ran, I spotted the big oak tree where I knew my bit of heaven was waiting for me. And there it was: a patch of blue with pink undertones sloping down to the fast- moving creek. The steep drop-off of the bank had protected the flowers from the cows. The exquisite beauty of each delicate little bell lining the stems and the pink buds below them blended into a perfect masterpiece.

All ten of us girls crowded into the carryall vehicle, each with flowers on her lap. We laughed and sang our way to Mount Moriah. We all crowded into the parlor upstairs in the old folks' area. The lady in charge played hymns, and we all sang around the piano. The old people sat smiling and nodding, and it crossed my mind that this was where my parents would soon live. The mood of the group buoyed me up, and if there were dark storm clouds on the horizon, I looked the other way.

Chapter 27
Choosing

Ed Freymiller was preaching on Sunday morning. He had been my favorite teacher since I discovered that I liked science and was good at it, and especially when I found bonus problems in the back of my chemistry book last year. Set A was challenging, and Set B was more challenging. Ed told me he didn't have time to solve them himself, but he would grade them for me. Each week, I lived for his words of praise as I aced the problems. I was overjoyed to find that my physics book this year had sets of bonus problems. Only Ed knew my secret that I was really good at solving problems. I must be really smart.

I sat up straighter in my folding chair as Ed opened his Bible on the homemade box that served as the pulpit. "As you know," he said, his voice warm with a subtle English accent from his childhood and missionary parents in India coloring his words, "you'll soon be leaving the safety of the school."

Of course we knew. My chest had been buzzing with anxiousness, anticipation, and fear in those last months of high school. That feeling made me lean into his words. "The world will not be friendly to you," he continued. "You girls are like hothouse plants."

Next to me, I felt Annie shift in her seat. My forehead furrowed. I had a vision of my father's little tomato seedlings, brilliantly green in the light that streamed in the east window in my bedroom in Union Grove. "You have been protected from worldly temptations," he continued. "You have been shielded from straying into bad habits."

I thought I had been preparing for the world, and now he was telling me I was still in the hothouse? I remembered my father telling me that the little plants needed to be slowly prepared for outdoors. When the days were mild, he would move the plants outside. At night, when the temperatures grew cooler, he would bring them in. They needed to be eased into the world— hardened off, he called it—so they could thrive in our garden.

Stop! I wanted to cover my ears. Ed's metaphor was frightening me. He sounded as if we were babies about to be dropped into a bleak and dangerous abyss. The truth was crashing over me—I wasn't prepared for the world. I had no access to books and no news except for the day Ed told us about *Sputnik*. I didn't know one woman with an ordinary job or a college education. My entire frame of reference was this place with its rules, its schedules, and its sermons.

I glanced around as discreetly as I could. My classmates were looking right at Ed. Did any of them feel as unsettled as I did? My thoughts spiraled back to fifth grade, flipping to the back page of my *Weekly Reader* to "Careers for Girls."

A stewardess? "Planes are dangerous," my mother said.

A telephone operator? Too confining.

A teacher or nurse? That meant training—a mystery to me. There were no jobs for me.

The school had taught us shorthand for secretarial work, but only to transcribe sermons. I was good at dictation, but my one and only D had been in typing. My fingers refused to hit the right keys. I would make a terrible secretary.

When Ed finally finished his analogy, I felt the prick of tears behind my eyes and a lump in my throat. I had been tricked into thinking I was ready for life after high school. It was dawning on me that I was prepared for one thing only—a canvassing home, obeying orders from the church, a single lady selling literature for the rest of my life.

As we stood for the closing hymn, my hands trembled as I held the hymnal, and the words of the song blurred. I needed to talk to Gloria now, right at that moment, but I had to wait until after the noon meal, which I did not even taste. When the dishes were done, I went straight to Gloria's room.

"Miss Whipple," I burst into her room. My agitation had returned, and my voice shouted urgency. "I feel like no one has given me a choice about my future. I saw in the school paper that Lynne has joined the church. Why hasn't anyone asked me to join? And in his sermon today, Ed Freymiller called us hothouse plants."

"Slow down," Gloria said, beckoning me to sit on her bed. "You already belong to the church. That's why you were not asked."

I remained standing. "What if I don't want to belong to the church? I'm a hothouse plant because I've been sheltered here with rules and prayer meetings so I can't do anything except become a canvasser for the church. Tell me I'm not right."

"We all have choices," Gloria said. "You have a choice to follow God's Plan for your life or turn away from God. I think we should pray."

I didn't move.

Gloria spoke up. "Why don't you go to your room and make a list. In one column write 'God's Plan' and in a second column write 'Other Choices.'"

I wanted to argue, but of course I didn't have other choices. I turned and left to make my list. "Come back and show me when it's finished," Gloria called after me.

I loved my sister, and I knew my words upset her. I drew two columns on my notebook paper. "God's Plan," I wrote. I didn't know what to call the second column, but not "Other Choices." Under "God's Plan" I wrote "Church," and under that I wrote "Heaven." Finally, I labeled the second column "The World." Under that heading was one word: "Hell."

Although I didn't yet know the term *brainwashing*, I realized I was untrained to live in the world.

Gloria read what I had written, and I knelt beside her on the bare wooden floor in her room to pray. My tears fell as I relinquished my dreams, my independence, and my sense of self to follow God's Plan.

Gloria praised the Lord, and her happy tears made me cry harder in my despair. As graduation neared, I rallied to the challenge and became consumed with my commitment to walk into my future with all the guardrails in place.

In my room, I looked at the gifts I received for graduation. My parents gave me a gold Bulova wristwatch, similar to those they had gifted my three older sisters on their graduation days. As I slipped it onto my wrist, I knew it was the most beautiful thing I had ever owned. It was so shiny and beautiful that wearing it almost seemed like a sin.

My oldest sister, Glady, sent me a gift: a mint green slip with matching panties. I wondered how she knew I was graduating. The last time I saw her, I was five, and my father was pushing her out of our rooms at the Bible School and telling her to never come back.

I also received graduation cards from many church members, and most of them contained money. As my collection of dollar bills grew, I knew exactly what I wanted to purchase.

When I was six years old, I received my first Bible as a prize from the Bible School's Sunday school for winning the memorization contest. My mother would read passages to me, and after practicing with her, I'd run up the stairs to my Sunday school teacher's room to recite them. I used that Bible throughout high school, and it had grown worn and shabby.

Now, I wanted a Bible with a black leather cover and thin, crinkly pages with gold edges.

When I counted my money, I had $50, more than I had ever had. Though it took every penny, I purchased that Bible. Like my watch, the edge of the Bible caught the glinting summer sunlight and made me feel special.

I received another gift. My grandmother sent me $5.00 and with it a letter. This was my first letter from her since we left Connecticut when I was four years old. In her letter, she wrote that she had been sick and spent much of her time resting. She closed with, "Life is too short to spend on the things of the world. I'm glad God showed me when I was young that the only way to enjoy life was to give it entirely to Him."

Commencement day was perfect. Pink cabbage roses perfumed the air along the driveway, and a hedge of bridal wreath bowed down with branches of tiny white petals in the warm sunshine in front of the school. We had lunch before going to Mount Moriah for the ceremony. One of the ladies made little place cards for each of the four of us graduates at the table. Our names were printed in calligraphy, and a tiny yellow rose from the bush outside the kitchen window was attached to each card.

In my green dress, I stood in front of the audience of parents and church members, ladies from the canvassing homes, and old people. I gave the valedictory address, an honor whose distinction was lost in the context of our tiny class. We had decorated an arch that hung over my head with our motto—A CHARGE TO KEEP I HAVE—in blue and silver block letters.

Near the end of my speech I spoke of the deepest desires of my soul: "Our first and greatest charge is to glorify God as we come to the end of our school days. We realize that we have had many more opportunities and advantages than the majority of young people of today. May God help us to accept the grave responsibility this places upon us."

Scrawled across the bottom of my diploma was one signature: Mr. Hitchcock. He was not there. He seemed to have been suddenly replaced by a new leader, Mr. Leon Graham, which was surprising. He was the preacher I had irked when I was eight years old and squirming in my seat at Lake Geneva. He gave the commencement speech. His charisma and strong message filled my heart with the resolve to follow God's plan into the church. And yet the question lingered: Was this really God's plan?

Chapter 28
South Chicago

From the start, I had no personal goals. My life was shaped by the expectations of the church. My parents raised us for the church. We would either join the church or leave for the world, in which case we were dead to the family. Kneeling with Gloria that Sunday afternoon at the end of my senior year, I realized that I had no other choice but to join the ranks of church canvassers. I had no money, no way to get money, no idea how to get a job, and no place to go.

The summer after graduation, Annie and I embraced our canvassing experience. We were roommates in a rented upstairs apartment on Chicago's South Side, canvassing as partners across the street from each other. The rest of the crew dropped us off in the mornings and picked us up at lunchtime and quitting time. We wore white hats and gray uniforms. For colder weather, we were issued dark gray suits. For half the year, our winter suits were hidden beneath our coats. My green coat had been a hand-me-down in high school, and none of the other women were dressed any better.

On Saturday afternoons, Annie and I sat on our beds tallying up our sales for the week, subtracting expenses and our $4.00 allowance. I looked at my profit with pride but knew better than to compare it with Annie's. She plodded along, going whole days with only one or two sales. In the weekly church paper, the *Bulletin*, canvassers were recognized with asterisks according to profit. If I wasn't in the highest bracket, I was disappointed.

That year, Grandma, my father's mother, wrote me again from Connecticut. "I just got a letter from your dad today," she wrote. Hmm, so he was writing to her. That explained why I got a card from her for graduation. She continued, "He says he hopes to be able to come out here this summer. I think he ought to, as we're old people now, and he's liable not to see us again if he doesn't come pretty soon." She ended her letter with, "Tell Auntie Hannah hello for me. With lots of love, your Grandma."

Auntie Hannah was our housekeeper. Her Bible School history reached back almost as far as my grandmother's. In South Chicago, she cooked our meals and prepared the lunches I looked forward to while pounding the pavement. Lunches always included homemade cookies or dessert bars alongside our sandwiches. Auntie Hannah had been the housekeeper for the first old folks' home in Union Grove when I was eight. On the coldest days, I would go there for lunch since it was only a block from school and home was over the railroad tracks, half a mile away.

It was during one of those wintertime lunches in Union Grove that Auntie Hannah spoke words I never forgot. Leon Graham was there that day. She patted his shoulder and said she had prepared a special meal for him. "He is God's precious young man," she said.

Aren't women special too? I wondered.

Ed Freymiller was now running the business part of the church from an office in a Chicago ally. The previous person in that role had followed Mr. Hitchcock to Denver. I finally understood that when

Leon and two other board members voted Mr. Hitchcock out – just before my high school graduation – the church had split again. My parents had not followed Mr. Hitchcock this time. They were lining up behind Leon Graham, our new president. Ed Freymiller was now the vice president and also the treasurer.

Every year, there was an annual canvassing contest. The canvasser with the highest earnings for the year got a prize. That year when I was in Chicago, Leon Graham presented me that prize—a small blue suitcase—at a little alley church in Chicago.

When the annual church convention rolled around in August, I found myself completely captivated by our new church leader, God's "special young man," Leon Graham. I listened to his sermons with rapt attention. If I'd learned one thing from my childhood in the Bible School and from my father's example, it was that the approval of the church leader was the most valuable thing you could have. Sitting there, surrounded by aging women in various stages of grace, I formed a plan. After the sermon, I marched up to the pulpit and waited in line to talk to Leon Graham.

"I want to learn Greek so I can study the Bible better," I said in my most sincere voice. Aware that others were waiting, I turned and joined the congregation who were leaving the room. Whatever Leon was expecting to hear from me, the look on his face told me I had surprised him with my words.

Leon handed out appointments at the end of the convention, and we learned that the South Chicago home was closing and the canvassers were being split up. "Please let me stay with Annie," I prayed.

Chapter 29
Back to Union Grove

I was assigned to Union Grove where I would live with two older church canvassers, Clara and Eleanor. Annie would be going somewhere else. I tried to see it in the best light possible. I would be near Leon since his family had moved into our old house. I would be noticed. Maybe he would let me study Greek. I could play with his children in the home where I had spent so much time growing up with my sister.

In South Chicago, I gathered my few possessions and hugged Annie tightly. She was heading to Race Street, the church home in Chicago, to canvass with her older sister. I felt the lump in my throat grow, and my final goodbye faded as I hurried into the car and headed for Wisconsin.

I was well acquainted with both of my new roommates. Clara's thin, blonde hair was pulled tightly into a bun, and her face was lined from years of working in the weather peddling literature for the church. She had even lived in our Union Grove home for a while, canvassing for the church, until my parents left for Mount Moriah to manage the old folks' home. My mother said she lived with us because she didn't get along well with the other canvassers. When the Grahams moved into the house, Clara and Eleanor rented an upstairs apartment together a couple blocks away on the street that ended at the town dumps.

I had rubbed elbows with Clara in the summers when I was home. One summer she took my mother, Linda, and me to a cabin on Lake Superior for a vacation. I had watched the sun rise over an island and turn the water into ribbons of orange and gold. I took my Bible down to the rocks along the shore and worshiped in the beauty of it all. During the summer before my senior year of high school, I had canvassed with her to earn my tuition—$150. It was something I wanted to do. I had no problems with Clara.

Eleanor, our crew leader, was a different story. I had also known her since we moved into our house in Union Grove when I was eight. She rented an old house on Main Street for an old folks' home, and my mother had helped her paint and fix it up while Linda and I played in the overgrown jungle at the back of the house. I sighed as I thought of Eleanor. Though she was my mother's friend, Linda and I usually stayed far away from her. She was a tall, broad German woman with coal-black hair twisted into a bun at her neck. Her face showed no smile lines, and I never heard her laugh.

Eleanor took my mother, Linda, and me to a park in Kenosha, Wisconsin, one evening. I ran off to play as usual. When I tried to jump over a small stream, I slipped. I grabbed a branch hanging over my head and learned about weeping willows that night. The branch lowered me into the water and laid me down on my back. I ran back to the car with dripping wet hair, shoes, and everything in between—all from a stream a few inches deep. My mother was horrified. I could not get into Eleanor's car like that. Eleanor found some papers for me to sit on, and my mother tried to wring the water from my dress. I was afraid of Eleanor's grim look that night.

Now, I was moving into Clara and Eleanor's upstairs apartment on the street only a couple blocks from the dumps. I carried my little blue suitcase into my room, which was just large enough for a single bed and chest of drawers. As I unpacked, I thought about supper and realized there was no housekeeper. Who would cook?

That night I found out. We each cooked two evening meals per week and made our own breakfast and lunch. I had never been comfortable in the kitchen and couldn't remember ever cooking an entire meal. My mother had a cookbook, and I had made corn fritters for the family, but here there was no cookbook. Later that winter, when the grease in my frying pan caught fire, Eleanor rushed in, opened the window, and threw the flaming pan out into the snow. I climbed on top of the stove to clean the greasy black layer of soot on the walls and ceiling but couldn't reach the corners. Somehow Eleanor got it clean, but I carried the guilt of that fire every time it was my turn to cook.

My first visit to my old Union Grove home was for Sunday dinner after church. Eleanor, who was Mrs. Graham's older sister, shooed me away when I wanted to play with the children. At the dinner table, I felt closer to the children's age than the adults. I listened silently as we ate broccoli with cheese. The conversations buzzed around me. After the meal, Clara and I washed up while the family went upstairs to settle the children for a nap. As we were about to leave, I saw Leon and asked the questions that were on my mind.

"Do your children like the doll buggy we left for them?" I asked.

He looked puzzled before answering. "It was old," he paused. "We had to get rid of it."

Something in me crumbled, but I pressed on. "Do you still have our big orange cat?"

"No," he said. "We had to get rid of him too."

I turned and walked out, unable to face him without breaking down.

My weekends settled into a pattern. Clara and I had the apartment to ourselves on Saturday and Sunday afternoons, but I had nothing to do. We ate Sunday dinner with the Grahams and walked home together afterward. Going for walks was out of the question. I was terrified someone would recognize me from my former life in Union Grove and I'd have to explain what I was doing there again. Eleanor would visit her family on Saturday afternoons and stay late on Sundays.

Eleanor had her own church car, and I worked with Clara and rode in her church car. On a day in late September, Clara and I were canvassing in one of the lake towns of southern Wisconsin. The morning began with warm sunshine casting shadows from red and yellow trees as the colored leaves floated down in the light breeze. Most of the lake cottages were already closed for the season, and the women who could afford what we were selling had returned to the cities. My sales were few and far between.

The Grahams were leaving for vacation that morning to Michigan. The thought tormented me. I would have managed better if the sun had stayed out, but clouds rolled in and the breeze morphed into a cold wind off the lake. I shivered in my gray cotton uniform. Dark thoughts crept in. I realized I would never be able to take a spontaneous trip like the Grahams. Worse, I would never have a husband or a family to take such a trip with. I would never get to plan fun or interesting things or choose my job. I felt doomed to become an old maid like Eleanor and Clara. Whenever a young mother answered a door with her baby or toddlers peeking around her, my heart wept. I knew it was God's Plan for women to support the church. Marriage would mean fewer resources for missions, the church school, and the elderly.

As I waited for Clara at the end of the day, my eighteen-year-old brain boiled with anger. My life stretched out ahead of me as a never-ending cycle of canvassing and church, nearly every dollar handed over to the institution. The more I sold, the more trapped I felt. God's Plan began to feel horrible and fiendish. I kicked at the piles of fallen leaves. As mist turned to droplets of rain that splattered my face, I saw Clara's old church car approaching. I slammed the back door after tossing in my canvassing bag and then slid into the passenger seat, wiping my face with my sleeve.

In the following weeks, I smiled less and spent most of my free time alone in my room. I wrote letters to my family but never expressed my true feelings. Sometimes I wanted to write my feelings all out in a journal, but that felt too risky. I began to wonder if Eleanor's aloofness was payback for the years I had avoided her as a child. A few years later at the school, she stopped me and asked me to forgive her. I told her I did, but I was never sure what I had forgiven her for.

Whether it was Eleanor or Leon who noticed my condition, it was Eleanor who came to me one day with a surprising suggestion.

"Would you like to get a puppy?" she asked. "You could get one from the Humane Society."

Though I hadn't wanted a dog, I knew something needed to change. I found a little brindle-colored beagle mix and named him Pebbles. He quickly became my confidant. I whispered my heart to him at night. But during the day, when I couldn't watch him, he escaped from my room through the old door that wouldn't latch.

A few weeks later, as Pebbles bounded up to greet me one evening, Eleanor stopped me. She pointed to the legs of the old table and chairs.

"Do you see what your dog has done?" Her voice sent terror through me.

I looked. The wood was scratched and gnawed by sharp puppy teeth.

"I've given you several chances to keep your dog in your room," she said. "You'll have to take him back to the Humane Society tomorrow morning."

My eyes blurred as Pebbles hopped between the front and back seats on my way to the Humane Society in Racine. I walked through the door, placed him on the counter, and ran out without a word. I made it to the car, drove a few blocks, and then the sobs took over—loud, shoulder-shaking, gut-deep sobs. I wailed into the emptiness of the car. Pebbles was gone.

Chapter 30
English 101

"You may be wondering why I brought you to Union Grove," Leon said, pulling me aside one winter day.

Yes, yes, I wanted to say. Why am I here?

"It's so you can attend a night class at the teachers' normal school. Of course, you'll have to wait for the January semester."

Whether it had been his plan all along or an attempt to rescue my drowning soul, I found myself at the normal school on a January night. I was twenty years old. It was 1961. A teacher's certificate could be earned in two years but I had no such goal.

It had snowed that day, and the path was slippery as I walked timidly to the front door of the school. I looked at the girls on their way to becoming teachers. My mind mocked the idea that it would ever be my path. I was just a puppet following orders.

It had been years since I left Union Grove after seventh grade, a chubby little girl with red-brown braids down her back. I had slimmed down, but the braids remained. The other girls at the teaching school wore slacks and sweaters. I pulled my worn coat over my cotton dress. This was my childhood repeating itself; I was the Holy Jumper in the room.

The chatter stopped when the teacher entered. He was an older man with white hair and a plaid jacket. Would he notice me, stiff in a sea of smiling faces? My breath caught as he called

roll.

"Doris Whipple."

"Present," I whispered. No heads turned. I exhaled.

The teacher described the English course. The girls pulled out notebooks and pencils. I opened my two-ring binder and began to copy the list on the blackboard. It was a list of required reading.

"If you've read them, refresh yourselves on your notes," he said.

Had I read them? I didn't recognize a single title. But he mentioned the Racine library. They had copies.

In that moment, my world shifted. I could sign up for a library card. The next day, I brought home an armful of books. One was on sex education, a subject I desperately needed to understand. I tucked it under my bed, buried beneath the other books.

But when I came home from work the next day, something felt off. Someone had been in my room. The books were rearranged. The sex education book was no longer at the bottom. I was pitched back into the darkness I'd been trying to escape.

Halfway through the course, the teacher assigned a term paper. I bought onion-skin paper and asked Leon for a typewriter. He found an old one, like the ones we'd used at the Potomac school. I was no better at typing, and my fingers kept missing the keys.

Chapter 31
Grandma

In April, as the snow began to melt, my father called. Long-distance calls were rare, so I knew something had happened. "Grandma died," he said. "Get on the next train. We're leaving for the funeral today."

Questions erupted, but he hung up.

Eleanor drove me to the train station in Racine. Gloria was waiting for me when I stepped off the train in Chicago, and we drove to Mount Moriah. Her face was sad. "Grandma was eighty," she said as we drove. "We should have visited sooner."

I bit my tongue. Did we ever have a choice?

At Mount Moriah, we all piled into the car, my little blue suitcase wedged in with the others. My mother sat beside my father in front, and Linda, Gloria, and I shared the back. My mother passed around sandwiches wrapped in wax paper, but they stuck in my throat. By nightfall, we reached the mountains on the Pennsylvania Turnpike. My father was hunched over the wheel, trailing the taillights of a semi.

"Slow down," my mother pleaded, but perversely, he inched closer. My sisters slept. I stared wide-eyed at the bouncing red lights in front of us, my world tilting with every swerve of the truck.

Morning light greeted us as we pulled up to my sister Glady's house. We changed into funeral clothes. The service that morning passed in a haze of hymns, unfamiliar faces, and sleepiness. At the cemetery, I scanned the crowd. These were aunts, uncles, and cousins, yet I recognized no one. I barely recognized my grandfather, but I couldn't miss him. He was a weathered, shrunken version of my father.

Later, we climbed the hill to my grandparents' home. Its weathered gray shingles and long, slanted roof had stood since the 1700s. Several generations of Whipples had lived there. My grandfather was living there when he courted my grandmother in 1898.

I watched cousins closest to my age. One of them climbed into a car with other young people, her short hair bobbing in the breeze. A boy was driving. A knife stabbed through me. When had I ever had such freedom? My youngest cousin darted in and out of the house, blending in while I stood apart.

The next morning, we gathered for a photo on Glady's stoop. Linda and I were strangers in the family group. Years later, I studied that image—my brother Floydie's squared shoulders, Gloria's forced smile, my own sad eyes. Only two family photos exist: this one and one from when I was three—fragments of a family pretending to be whole.

After we drove back to Mount Moriah, I caught a train back to Union Grove. My grief erupted. I muffled sobs into my coat. A man offered to pay my fare. An older woman touched my arm.

"Can I help?" she asked.

I shook my head. No one could help me. I had seen the world, and it was not what I had been taught. My sisters and brother were loving and kind. My cousin could go out with boys. My grandmother had loved the Lord until the end.

Slowly, anger burned through my grief. My father had been wrong to keep me from my grandparents, to banish my two sisters and my brother. Nothing could mend the chasm between us and our "sinful" relatives, not even the truth curdling inside me. What if the church was wrong? What if there was no Plan?

Chapter 32
Kicking Rocks

In May, I sat at the dining table in the upstairs apartment, typing my term paper. It covered absent fathers, shattered homes, Sunday school families, mission trips—their stories bled together. "Alcohalism"—I misspelled the title every time it appeared despite retyping page after page to correct other typing mistakes. When the A– paper came back, the grade felt hollow with the title circled in red.

That journey to Connecticut for the funeral had begun my unraveling. The threads were pulled—Grandma's death, my banished sisters and brother, the forbidden cousins. I had swallowed a lie that the world was a wicked place. The photograph taken on my sister's porch haunted me. We weren't a family; we were wreckage, scattered by a doctrine that confused control with salvation.

The week after our trip to Connecticut, I sensed something was not right with me. My breakdown on the train threatened to spill into every moment of the day. I was canvassing like an actor on a stage. My face ached after every day of forced smiles. I was saying the words, but I was not truly present.

I stopped Leon at church on Sunday morning. "I need to talk to you," I said. I sounded like a desperate child yearning for attention. I told him I wanted to discuss the Holy Ghost. He would be more likely to listen to that than to questions about why the church controlled our personal lives.

After Sunday dinner at the Graham house, I went into the parlor to wait for Leon. There had never been a door in the doorframe, and the curtains my mother had hung were gone. I sat down on the couch. Glancing around, the room seemed frozen in time. I was sitting on our old couch—I would know my mother's flowered slipcovers anywhere. Her piano still stood in the corner, pushed up against the unused door to the porch. It was a room that held memories, both sweet and aching, and as I sat there, homesickness washed over me like a tide.

When Leon finally entered, he sat down beside me. I shifted closer, my voice low, eager to keep our conversation private. The women in the house were nearby, their chatter drifting in from the kitchen.

I began to speak, but my voice cracked almost immediately. I took a deep breath, steadying myself. "I want to talk about my sisters and brother," I said. "My grandparents were not bad people; my sisters and brother are not bad people. Why did my father cut them off? It seems like everyone in our church has relatives on the outside. Are we on the inside the only ones going to heaven?"

There. I had said it, not the Holy Ghost conversation he expected but the cry of my heart, now lying exposed in all its brokenness. Before he could reply, his wife appeared in the doorway. I hadn't noticed her approach, but I felt Leon stiffen. Her voice was firm and commanding. "Leon, I need you to come help with the children right now." He stood up quickly, and I realized how closely we had been sitting, our thighs pressed together, our heads bent in quiet conversation. "You've got to go home," she said to me, her gaze cold and fixed.

My heart leapt into my throat as confusion, then shame, and then anger flushed my cheeks with a throbbing heat. The counseling I needed so badly would not happen today. Without a word, I let myself out and started up the road, the same road I had walked countless times as a child, the road where my father had chased me when I wanted to go to the movies. The familiarity of it should have been comforting, but instead, I was overwhelmed by a suffocating wave of revulsion. My chest tightened, my breath came in shallow gasps, and my heart raced. There were no tears, just anger threatening to take my breath away.

I had looked to Leon as a father figure, but now he loomed over my life as a source of pain. He had ordered me here, controlled my path, and left me to endure numbing misery for a year. I kicked at the gravel beneath my feet, the only release I could find. Loose rocks scattered across the path ahead. I kicked again, harder this time, my frustration and grief spilling out in each motion. I wanted to scream, to let the world know how broken I felt, but all I could do was kick at the ground and mutter, "I don't believe it. There is no Holy Ghost." I dared not say God's name, but I was furious with Him.

How could the loving God I'd learned about all my life leave me so isolated and alone? I kicked another rock, allowing the burden of my sadness to play out in the power of anger. As I stood there, feelings raging, the road ahead seemed endless, and I was alone, grappling with the emptiness that had taken root in my heart.

Chapter 33
Classes

"You'll be going to Race Street after Linda's graduation," Eleanor told me. I assumed Leon had ordered it, but why now? Were Eleanor and Clara so tired of me that they demanded I be moved before the convention appointments at the end of August?

"Okay," I mumbled. I didn't ask questions. I would be happy to leave Union Grove, whatever the reason.

I was looking forward to a break for Linda's high school graduation in Potomac. Now I was not to return to Union Grove, but to go to the church's main canvassing home in Chicago run by Helen Schedel. Everyone liked Helen. She was as close to a saint as anyone I knew. I would have no problems with her. Her smile touched the places where a boost was needed and she was often called to sort out any problems with the canvassers.

Linda's graduation was a milestone that should be celebrated with flowers and fireworks—well, flowers at least; fireworks weren't appropriate for graduations. During kindergarten and her first four years of elementary school, Linda attended only a few weeks in the fall and again when the weather was warm in the spring. My mother was a good teacher, and Linda learned reading, writing, and arithmetic at home during the winter months. By fifth grade, she'd grown stronger, walking to school and back daily except on cold, rainy days or when snow was deep. It was a triumph of improved health and my mother's prayers that she completed each school year. Even during the Asian flu, which sent every girl to bed battling fever and congestion, Linda pulled through without a night vigil.

"Please don't make her canvass," I prayed. She could not lug heavy bags or climb steps in humid summers and icy winters. What would she do? When I returned to the old folks' home (I refused to call it "my" home), I asked my mother about Linda's future.

"She'll be staying here," she answered. "I can always use the help until something else opens up for her."

What could "open up" in our church for a seventeen-year-old with a congenital heart defect? Was it anger, helplessness, or rebellion I felt toward my parents in that moment? So, Linda would live in the old folks' home. She had no more choice about her future than I did.

Race Street in Chicago was my third canvassing home in two years. It was the oldest and largest home in the church. Over the years, I'd visited and noticed women who'd been canvassing longer than I'd been alive. I hoped Annie would be there, but she'd been sent to the Potomac school to help can vegetables.

"Are you excited to take another college course?" Helen, the crew manager, asked when I arrived at Race Street. This was the first I'd heard of it. She handed me a booklet of course offerings from Wright Junior College. Though I'd earned an "A" at the normal school, the emotional toll of perfectionism and being "out in the world" with no clue how to fit in had nearly broken me. I wanted to protest that this was a waste of time and money when I had no plans to use it. Still, I flipped through the booklet, seeking classes on Fridays or Saturdays. The only option without prerequisites was another English class.

"I've already taken English," I told Helen.

"But this one will be different," she insisted.

I registered and bought the required *Webster's Dictionary*. It would have helped when I misspelled the title of my term paper. If nothing else, this dictionary was mine, and I could write my name in it. I rubbed my fingers across the glossy paper cover.

The days before my class began were sweltering. The city steamed. There was no respite when the canvassing day ended, and I retired to the stuffy attic room I shared with an older woman. Every morning, it seemed I had to pick up my spirit where it lay on the ground. As I canvassed, my feet marched to the rhythm of my screaming thoughts: This isn't the life I want. I want out now! And then I formed a plan.

On Friday afternoon, near quitting time, I stopped at a corner store. "A pack of Camels," I told the cashier. I hid the cigarettes in my pocket and climbed into the car as usual, but my plan was set. For the first time in ages, I felt hope.

On Saturday afternoon, wearing a green and pink hand-me-down dress and clutching my dictionary, I entered Wright Junior College's courtyard. I chose a stone bench, opened my purse, and noticed students laughing nearby. Three boys drifted toward me as I fumbled with the cigarette pack. I panicked, stood abruptly, and walked toward my car. Not to be completely defeated, I lit a cigarette and stepped into the street. I coughed. I threw the cigarette down and stomped it out. It was just as bad as I had been warned.

Once class let out, I went back to the canvassing home. That night, I confessed to Helen, "I didn't go to class. I smoked a cigarette." Horror flashed across her face as if I'd marched straight into hell. On Sunday, I boarded a train to go back to my parents in Potomac. They didn't question me. To my shock, I'd be a counselor again at girls' camp.

The truth was that the young people were not falling into place the way Leon needed them to. The system was breaking down. All the Lake Geneva graduates except two had left for "the world," and the three girls who graduated in Potomac shortly after I graduated quit canvassing within weeks. God's plan for young lives to be spent canvassing was looking grim, and now, with few prepared for real jobs and even fewer willing to stay, Leon had to come up with something to do with those who remained. Linda needed a place, and no canvassing home wanted to take me on.

Years earlier, the Bible School had offered a seminary for adults called Classes. My parents had attended. Now Leon announced that Classes would begin that fall, this time for recent high school graduates.

Leon and his family had left Union Grove and moved to Potomac. The church had bought them a house there so Leon could run things at the school. Ten of us made up the Classes group—eight girls, including Linda and me, and two boys. Linda dreaded the thought of going back to school so soon after graduating. I was reluctant, too, still feeling like a bird caught in the church's net.

The high school students had dwindled to a handful, and that fall the Classes students moved back into the dorms with them. Linda and I each had our own room in the gray building on the side closest to the farm buildings.

On Monday morning, we gathered in an upstairs room in the school building, now our dedicated space. Leon began by asking, "What do you want to study this year?"

Someone suggested the Bible. After five years of Bible study in high school, this wasn't at the top of my list. We could have more Spanish classes, given Leon's fluency. I raised my hand. "I want to learn more about human biology."

He tasked me with drawing the human body on a portable blackboard and labeling its parts. When he examined my work, he paused, and with an embarrassed sigh, he instructed me to adjust the proportions of the male anatomy. With no textbooks, the class ended after a test on the names of body parts. I fell back into my high school study habits, acing Bible lessons and Spanish while seeking out the teacher's approval.

Thrown back into the sheltered Christian atmosphere of the school, I faced a choice: continue my rebellion or recommit to God and the church. I knew rebellion would mean a catastrophic rift with my family. Now, needy and desperate, I began writing letters to Leon: "I am trying to resolve my rebellion and find God's Plan," I scribbled.

Leon made time for me whenever I wrote, offering counsel and prayers. His attention became my oxygen, my reason to realign with God and the church.

Chapter 34
Looking Around

On Thanksgiving at the old folks' home with our parents, my mother dropped a bombshell. "Gloria is getting married," she said, "to Ed Freymiller." Linda and I stared, speechless.

"When?" we blurted out together.

"At Christmas," she answered.

The last I knew, Gloria was still in Brownsville, Texas, doing missionary work, while Ed was living in a garage in a Chicago alley, managing church business. How were they even dating?

My mother bought Linda and me matching blue dresses for the wedding. She baked a two-tier cake with pink and white icing. The ceremony was held in the schoolroom with the "God Is Love" engraving. Gloria and Ed stood by the piano as Leon officiated, witnessed only by the old folks and school staff. Afterward Gloria moved to the Chicago alley with Ed. Linda and I went back to Classes.

The church was changing, but since we were tucked away in Classes, it almost passed us by. With Mr. Hitchcock gone, Leon was dismantling the most sacred tenet of the church: celibacy. Couples were pairing up, and Leon was not only giving his approval but also marrying them. Since women outnumbered men by a huge ratio, there were still enough spinster canvassers to support the school, missions—and the Graham family.

If I stayed in the church, and it was looking like I would, I had to act fast. There were only two eligible young men in Classes, and David was my choice. He had been two grades ahead of me in high school but was closest to my spot on the honor roll and had beaten me in more than one oratorical contest. During spring canvassing at the school, he had outsold me for the largest sale of the day. I was pretty sure we would see eye to eye if we could just get together.

When we entered the cafeteria for breakfast on the first day of the annual convention, I scanned the room for David. My plan worked. Soon, his eyes sought me out during meals. We continued our game. When our gazes locked, a chill ran down my spine. The jolt was addicting. This was fun until one day when Leon stood behind me during a prolonged eye lock and whispered in my ear, "I can see what you're doing, and it's disgusting." Of course he would say that, but how else was I supposed to secure my future? I was navigating my destiny. Nevertheless, our glances ceased.

David and I resumed our connection the only way we could. When Leon left the classroom, David would wiggle his prominent ears at me and, of course, I'd grin.

Chapter 35
Icy Roof

One frigid January evening, the snow lay unmelted since New Year's, crusted ice coating everything. I sat on my bed, leaning against the outer wall, when I thought I heard Linda calling. I opened the window, and a cold blast hit my face. She called again. I raced downstairs, out the kitchen door, and to the driveway beneath our windows. There she lay, facedown on the icy ground, blood spattered around her head. I screamed for help and ran to call Leon. When the ambulance left to take Linda to the hospital, I alerted our parents but declined Leon's offer to follow the ambulance with him.

I couldn't process what had happened. My lifelong role had been to protect Linda. What if I hadn't heard her through the wall? Why had she done something so reckless? What if she'd died?

Her window was open when I entered her room. Outside, the porch roof sloped beneath a layer of ice. The ceiling light glinted off the frozen shingles. My emotions swung between grief at nearly losing her and fury at her foolishness.

Our relationship had been damaged once before. She'd written to me after I was sent to Potomac. "You upset me awfully when you acted as you did," she wrote. "I despise that awful spirit in myself, and my whole nature will despise you, too, if you don't stop it." She'd signed off sweetly: "I do love you lots." Her words had pierced me then, but now, whatever her reason for stepping out on the roof, she'd been the one to disrupt the bond we shared. Why?

The next morning, my mother called. Linda had survived the night. Her fractured elbow was set, and the blood on the snow had come from cuts caused by her shattered glasses. She was awake and talking.

I didn't probe about why she'd climbed onto the roof. The answer wouldn't come for another year. She didn't return to Classes.

By the end of the school year, Linda was at High Desert Mission in Gallup, New Mexico, founded for Navajo outreach. She thrived there, feeling part of Christian work. As in high school, she gravitated toward animals. She wrote, "Bigi (a goat) is nimble. He jumped to the top of my dresser today and stared at himself in the mirror!"

And in classic Whipple fashion, she wrote, "Last Wednesday, Bigi and I hunted flowers for Mrs. Hill's May basket. The early blooms are tiny—smaller than violets. I found six kinds and arranged them in a pretty little box."

Linda had upset me, but I still loved her fiercely. When she returned for August convention, our sisterly bond remained unbroken.

Chapter 36
More Classes

The second year of Classes grew repetitive. Three girls were gone; we were down to a total of five. Bored by heavy study, Leon devised a new plan. We'd visit Sunday schools and church missions with singing and acting programs.

In November, we piled into the carryall for our first trip to High Desert Mission in New Mexico. The boys claimed the front seats, taking turns driving. With a faulty heater, the back seats were stacked with quilts. Leon sat in the center in the middle row. Whenever I wedged myself against the door beside him, a thrill buzzed through me. I felt special. My mood lifted.

During a gas station break, he pulled me aside. "Always get in last, after me," he said.

I obliged happily. That day, under the quilt, his hand brushed mine, and my breath caught. Holding hands beneath the quilt became our ritual. He was bothered that I liked David, but now I knew I was in his head. I was special. I mattered. It was not all bad. Was he one-upping David, who was driving?

I marveled at High Desert's missionary culture. At services, Leon preached, and a young man interpreted his sermons into the Navajo language. Benches were filled with women in velvet blouses, long skirts, and turquoise jewelry. Fewer men attended, but there were more than I'd ever seen in our church. They were dressed in work shirts, jeans, and cowboy boots. Young mothers sat with children on their laps, a sight foreign to my experience.

My twenty-first birthday arrived before our departure. At breakfast, Leon spoke to the director in front of the group. "Do you have a rug we can give Dorie for her birthday?"

I caught Mrs. Hill's surprised expression at the request. Older Navajo women wove rugs to support their families; hers were treasured gifts. She emerged with a vibrant red rug, woven with the words *Jesus Saves* in a white cross down the middle. It was too beautiful for me, but I accepted it graciously.

Back in Potomac, Linda continued my birthday with a card and a poem she had written in green and pink pencil.

Happy Birthday Sister

A birthday is a time of cheer
But as you start another year,
I know it won't be all that way.
Some days you're sure to be upset
With more than one could ever do,
But always you will have a friend,
'Cause you have me, and I have you.

The sky may oft be overcast,
Yet past the clouds, it still is blue.
And come what may, let's face the storm,
You still have me, and I have you.

I'm thankful for you, Sis.
God's plans are always for the best.
Though friends may fade and dreams may crash,
We need not fear, for God is true.
He's proved His great and gracious love,
He gave you me, and gave me you.

With all my love,
Linda

Oh, Linda! Thank you for the poem.

Chapter 37
Trapped

After Gloria and Ed got married, they moved to Milwaukee where Ed took over as pastor of our church there. In February 1963, baby Grace Freymiller was born. Linda was staying with Gloria, and by Easter, I traveled north to meet the baby.

After cuddling Grace and helping tuck her into her crib in her parents' bedroom, Linda and I dragged our rollaway cots side by side into the living room. In her last letter, Linda had confessed, "I feel torn between a dozen things. Sometimes I don't know what I'm doing, what I'm supposed to do, or when. Nothing makes sense anymore—no pattern, no order."

"I know that feeling," I whispered. "The church . . . I don't think anyone knows what to do now. Leon wants me to teach at the high school next fall. I don't feel ready."

"Everything's just . . . one endless mess," she murmured into the dark. "I wish I had a plan, but it's all chaos." Her voice trembled, heavy with a sadness I could almost touch. She was voicing my own feelings. What could I say except agree?

A pause stretched between us before I gathered the courage to ask, "Why'd you go out on the roof last year?"

"I don't want to talk about it."

"Please," I pressed. "Why?"

She hesitated. "I shouldn't have, but I thought I heard someone calling me."

"Who?"

Her breath hitched. "Robert."

"The boys' superintendent?" I gasped.

"Shh! They'll hear you!" she warned.

"He'd call me at night," she whispered. "I'd sneak out to meet him."

My stomach dropped. Robert? He was way too old for her. She was seventeen, a child. What was he thinking? But even as outrage swelled, I understood. I was dealing with my own contradiction. Leon was more out of reach than Robert, and yet in that strange space he gave me solace. The church was drowning in loneliness. We were all aching for love, for family, and for a fulfilling life.

Lying there, waves of my own longing crashed over me. David had been drafted into the Army and was somewhere being trained, lost to me. Linda deserved someone her own age, someone free from the suffocating rules. We were trapped in this iron cage together, and it was the church.

"None of this is normal," I thought, staring into the shadows after the whispering stopped. The walls seemed to be closing in. I wanted to tear them down—for her, for me, for all of us.

Gloria helped Linda secure a job at a candy factory where she could work sitting down. Linda seemed thrilled, but then Linda wrote that someone at work mentioned that the University Hospital in Madison, Wisconsin, was performing successful patent ductus heart surgeries for free. I assumed she'd drop the idea, but her next letter was troubling. "I went to a heart doctor," she wrote.

"He told me I'm risking a heart attack before I'm twenty-five if I don't have surgery."

That shocked me, but I pushed it to the back of my mind and prepared for my trip to Denver at the end of the school year. I would stay with Great Aunt Jessie, my grandmother's sister, and her adult children. Her husband, my grandfather's brother, was Uncle John, the holy jumper who could do a handstand over the altar. He now lay buried in India where they'd served as missionaries with the Metropolitan Church. Missionary zeal ran strong in our family.

As I rode with a church family to Denver, a sign for Fort Leavenworth flashed by as we entered Kansas. "That's where David is!" I exclaimed, revealing more of my secret longing than I'd planned. "Can we stop to see him?"

The driver's response was gentle yet firm. "I don't think it's possible. The fort's big, and they aren't expecting us." Waves of disappointment washed over me. I'd lost David again.

Chapter 38
Unplanned

In Denver, a letter from Linda awaited me. I tore it open, paralyzed by fear as I read, "I made a duster, a dark blue floral trench coat. Mama will stay with me at the hospital, and Daddy will come and get us afterward. Aunt Jessie has my hospital address under 'Linda' in her book." My parents had approved the operation, and the date was set. My thinking stopped. How could I accept this? What if it wasn't successful? How did she persuade our parents?

My cousins in Denver were excited to see me, but my mind was elsewhere. I barely remembered to thank Great Aunt Jessie for the roast beef dinner, mistakenly calling it a "boiled dinner." I kicked myself for that later. Before heading to my basement room, I glanced at the church bulletin. I always checked the canvassers' rankings, and there it was: David's APO address. He'd been deployed to Vietnam. Even if we'd stopped in Kansas, I would've missed him. I grabbed a scrap of paper from the wastebasket and scribbled down his address.

That night, I wrote two letters—one to Linda and one to David. While my cousin Earle took us sightseeing in the mountains around Denver, Linda was undergoing surgery in Madison. My mother wrote that Linda was overjoyed her heart was beating normally for the first time. She was making plans for a "normal life."

"Happy birthday, Linda," I wrote. She celebrated her twentieth birthday in the hospital.

Meanwhile, David replied to my letter, and we wrote so often that our letters nearly crossed paths.

Then my mother called. "It's not going well," she said, her voice breaking. I could feel her tears over the telephone. "The patch on Linda's heart didn't hold. They took her back for emergency surgery, but now she's running a high fever."

My heart dropped. "What are you saying, Mama? Is she going to be okay?"

"We're praying, Dorie. It's all in God's hands. It's a long fight ahead." She paused. "I need to go home to catch up on business and wash my clothes. Can you come back to Wisconsin and stay with Linda?"

"I'll see you soon," I answered. "Tell Linda I'm coming."

I wanted to scream, to stop time. My world was collapsing. David's letters suddenly didn't matter. Guilt buried me for caring about his words while Linda fought for breath. Oh, Linda. "Please, God. Are You there? Do You know about this? Do You care?"

When I finally arrived at the hospital, my mother stood hollow-eyed and drained. We walked to Linda's room, and I prayed that the unwavering faith she carried for her youngest child might reach where mine couldn't. Linda was propped up in bed, her freckles pale against the white sheets. "Dorie!" She was excited when she saw me. I ran to hug her and then gasped. A huge tube was draining fluid from her chest. I swallowed my shock.

"I missed you," I whispered, squeezing her hand.

During the week I was there, I did everything to distract her. There was no radio and no television. We'd never had them, but the silence gnawed at me. I sang to her, and she joined in when she could. I tried to talk, but every topic hit a wall. I couldn't mention David. If she couldn't have a boyfriend, I couldn't share my hopes. Each day, the fever stole more of her breath and strength.

I read aloud from a book my mother had brought to the hospital, *Homesteading in Alaska*. My voice trembled. When the story turned humorous, I giggled and then laughed, the girlish laugh we'd always shared. "Stop," Linda said. "Stop laughing. It hurts."

"But it's funny," I argued.

"Stop!" she nearly yelled. Then it hit me. Linda couldn't laugh. The story wasn't funny anymore. My little sister couldn't laugh. Tears slipped from her eyes. I pulled my chair closer, my own tears falling. There were no words. I held her hand until she slept, and then I slipped out of the room.

When my mother returned, it was time for me to leave. I steeled myself. She'll get well. The fever will break. My goodbye isn't really goodbye. I wanted to wave—the "see you later" wave—but I didn't. I bent to kiss her, tears blocking my words.

"Don't cry, Dorie, I'm trusting Jesus," Linda said softly. "You trust Him too." Her hand reached for mine.

"I will," I choked.

Summer was winding down when I returned to Mount Moriah after my time with Linda. It was convention week. People were praying for Linda and stopped me to say they were praying for me as well. I was walking in a daze. "Why, God? You knew this would happen. You planned this, and now I have to live in Your mess."

I thought of David. His last letter lay unanswered in my suitcase. He wrote that he had scribbled my name all over his notebook. If only I had someone to talk to about him I might be able to bridge my feelings, but how could I dream of a happy future when Linda's had been stolen? A year ago, I had been reprimanded by Leon for flirting with David, so I knew better than to go to Leon. Miss Hey, my English teacher in high school, was the only teacher I felt could have held her own with college professors. She also preached, taking turns with Ed on Sunday afternoons. One afternoon during convention, I knocked on her door.

"Miss Hey," I said, kneeling beside her cot, "I've been writing to David."

"Oh, Dorie," she cut me off, "God has something so much better for you." We prayed, and I left. If I had expected counseling, there was none. Why? David had been a better Christian in our school days than I ever was. Surely she remembered my rebellious streak and my endless prayers for mercy. The prison bars of church celibacy slammed shut with a clank that afternoon.

My mother called the next week. I knew it was coming. My father and I left immediately for the hospital in Madison. Darkness had fallen when we arrived—darkness upon darkness. Gloria and Ed were already there, waiting with my mother. One by one, we went into Linda's room. Her eyes were closed, and her breathing was shallow. A small light over her bed cast long shadows across the room.

When I returned to the waiting room, I saw that my mother had collapsed into sobs. My father and sister Gloria were holding her. No one was with Linda. I slipped back into her room. Her breaths came in gasps. "She's almost gone," the nurse standing by whispered. I leaned in, reaching for her hand. "You don't have to do this alone, Linda." I kissed her. Her chest stilled.

Linda was my heart. With her gone, was there anything worth living for?

Chapter 39
Hug

In the following days, I often felt like an observer standing just outside the frame of our family's grief. Glady and Muriel came, not for Linda whom they had never known but to comfort our mother whom they still cherished. Floydie was there too; I recognized his quiet sorrow for the little sister he had tried to protect. Gloria, strong in her own way, had her husband and her daughter to hold onto. I struggled to find a space to mourn my own broken heart. Our family had ceased to be whole long ago when my father sent Glady away. Then Muriel left, and finally my brother, Floydie. We were together now for the funeral but there would be no family photos.

Leon drew me aside on the day of the funeral. "I bought a little sweetheart pillow for you to place beside her," he said. It was a white satin heart with tiny red rosebuds, wrapped in a ribbon that read "Sister." As I stared at it, something inside me shattered. Tears flowed uncontrollably. Leon reached out to me, and I leaned in, my head resting on his shoulder. I hugged him fiercely. But the closeness meant to comfort me left me feeling confused. I pulled away, sinking into a chair. That gesture became a source of guilt I couldn't shake. I needed comfort but from someone else, someone whose embrace wouldn't leave me feeling conflicted.

I gathered my school books and began my new career. I would be teaching at the school in Potomac that year. But teaching did nothing to assuage my devastation. If anything, my life, already aimless, felt entirely broken. There was no patch to mend my heart, just as no patch was able to save Linda.

I chose to stop writing to David since my unsettled relationship with Leon made me fear his disapproval. A year ago, Leon had rebuked me sharply, and Miss Hey had said it clearly: David was not part of God's plan for me. Despite my growing certainty that no divine plan had existed for Linda's life, I was afraid to abandon the thought that a plan might still exist for me. Relinquishing my box of lilac-scented stationery and David's letters to Leon marked the end of my dreams.

If a life has a defining moment, Linda's death was mine. Could joy ever return when she could never again experience it? Could I anticipate new experiences when she had been robbed of a future? Would my heart ever heal from this monumental grief? In my shadow mind, I envisioned Linda in heaven, free from pain and broken dreams, but the void of living without her was unfathomably deeper than I could have imagined. Dying seemed easier than living, and although I never pondered suicide, the thought of ceasing to exist, just fading out of the picture, crossed my mind frequently.

One day as I was packing up after school, Leon entered my classroom. "I want you to be my secretary," he said. "When school is out for the day, come to the typing room, and I will dictate church letters for you to transcribe and type up."

I had been avoiding my times with him when we would meet to pray. I had no desire to fake seeking God's will. I agreed to type his letters, but internally I seriously questioned my suitability for the role. Almost anyone would be better for the job than I was. At the start of the year when Leon's wife—the business teacher—had to be absent, she asked me to assist her typing student. I looked at the typing book and told the student to practice the home keys. When she returned, she confronted me. "You were supposed to give her timed drills," she said, her tone stern. It took me back to my own struggle with typing drills. I never wanted to face a typewriter again, yet Leon was asking me to be his secretary.

My shorthand was flawless, and sitting beside his desk for dictation was no problem. Once finished, Leon would sit at his desk while I headed to one of the old typewriters. As I attempted to type, the letter turned into a chaotic mess, words running together with only a phrase here and there that was readable. Rather than starting over, I continued the rapid tap, tap, tap on the keys until Leon left the room. Then I discarded the jumble and started fresh, painstakingly pressing each key, often needing to start over again.

One day, as I waited for him to leave, he spoke. "Dorie, I have a little note for you. Read it and then tear it up and throw it away." I took the paper from his hand. On it were five upper- case letters: ISALY. "I shall always love you," he explained. "Now tear it up." I dropped the torn pieces into the wastebasket as he watched.

Every day after that, I collected my note from his desk. It was always the same five letters. What kind of love was he imagining? One thing I felt sure of: It would be a sin to love him back.

As church members, we were almost never able to follow even the smallest fashion trend, but something had slipped under the radar. Girls had begun to wear little silk scarves under the collars of their blouses, knotted in the front. I had acquired a little red square which I folded and wore with every outfit that could tolerate bright red. One day I felt Leon's eyes on me as I sat typing. I looked up as he spoke.

"Since I have to leave to visit the mission fields tomorrow, I wonder if you will let me have your red scarf to put in my suitcase."

I untied the knot and slid it off. I walked up to his desk and held it out. I returned to my typewriter feeling something had transpired that wasn't quite right. He never gave my scarf back to me, and I never got another one.

Chapter 40
To Connecticut

As I neared the end of my second year of teaching, the same old angst returned, the kind that had overwhelmed me back in Union Grove. I felt stuck. My life was going nowhere. I was questioning the tenets I'd been taught. And on top of that, I was growing increasingly uncomfortable around Leon.

A new plan began to take shape. I thought of Glady, her graduation gift, the warm hug she gave me after Linda died. She had helped our sister Muriel escape the church. Maybe she would help me too. At the end of May 1964, I wrote her a letter. Not long after, I received a Western Union envelope with $60 for a train ticket to Connecticut.

The morning I left, my mother clung to me in a hug. How could I do this to her? She was losing another child. I ran outside to meet Leon, who had agreed to drive me to the train station. As we pulled away, he asked for my new address. I gave it to him. What he didn't know was that a large part of my decision to leave stemmed from his attention and the complicated pull of attraction that existed between us. He ran our church; he was God's voice in my life. He gave me orders. I felt trapped under his authority. I remembered the fractures in my family as my first sibling and then two more were driven away by my father.

After Leon dropped me at the station, I spotted a blue mailbox and slipped in a letter addressed to David. Was there still a tiny chance I could have him? The worst that could happen was that he'd ignore me or tell me to get lost. Either way, I was already lost, so why not try? I knew one thing: I couldn't have both David and the church. I gave him Glady's address in Connecticut—where I was going.

It was late afternoon when I arrived in Connecticut in the city where I was born. Twenty hours on the train, and Friday had slipped into Saturday. Glady was waiting for me at the train station.

I recognized her immediately. She had the same pretty face as our mother, with eyes and hair like the rest of us. She had green eyes the color of mine and light brown hair like Gloria's. I caught my breath. Would she think I looked strange or old-fashioned, like someone just crawling out of a cave? Then it hit me. Somewhere along the ride east, I hadn't just left a few states behind. I had left the church. I had entered the world I'd been taught to fear.

I stifled an exclamation of awe as we pulled into the driveway of the home my brother-in- law Elbert had built. On a corner lot, framed with tall evergreen trees, stood the house of my dreams. Around the stoop, bushes of pink flowers were blooming—rhododendrons, I later learned. The house was far newer than anyplace I had ever stayed. Across the road was the old farmhouse where I had lived the first four years of my life, now owned by another Whipple family.

This was the life I wanted, the world I wanted to live in. But could I ever belong? I lifted my little blue suitcase from the trunk of the car, aware that all it contained was worn-out clothes I had no money to replace. After spending the money on the ticket, I had less than $5 in my purse.

I shrank from the curious stares of my nephews and niece as I walked into the house. If I had seen them at my grandmother's funeral, I didn't remember. My niece was almost seventeen now, just six and a half years younger than I. She was cute, her short hair curled around her face. I hadn't had short hair since I was five and never curls, and I had no idea how to fix my hair like hers. Even as I hugged her, questions rolled around in my mind. Was she seeing how out of place I felt? Did she know that her world was as new to me as if I were a newborn? This was family, but I may as well have been dropped into a foreign country with unknown sights and sounds blurring out family.

On Sunday morning, the family went to church, but I stayed behind. After lunch, Elbert took the kids and me for a ride. I sat in the back seat beside my niece. Suddenly my heart dropped. The car had slowed down. We were turning into a Dairy Queen. I had never seen money exchanged on a Sunday in my life. I should tell him I didn't want anything, but that would cause a scene. I licked my ice cream with the rest of them and worried I would never fit into this world.

On Monday morning, I came upstairs to find Glady at the kitchen table, listening as her youngest read aloud. The bus came early for the older two children. I followed Glady around as she grocery shopped, cooked, and visited while avoiding the real reason I had turned up in her life.

On Tuesday, the letters started arriving. I carried them down to my room and sat on the bed. Without hesitation, I tore open David's letter first. "Please, God," I whispered. "Please let him be there for me."

"I am attending college at Ann Arbor, Michigan" he wrote, "and I have met the girl I'm going to marry."

My life kept falling apart—dream by dream, hope by hope. Of course he would move on. I had made it clear in my last letter that we were over.

I stared at the two remaining letters on the bed, one from Leon and the other from my mother. Neither of them would contain anything I wanted to read. I chose the one from Leon and scanned it. The five capital letters I knew so well jumped out at me: ISALY. And then the warning: Tear it up. When the last tiny pieces fluttered into the wastebasket, I turned to the third letter. I didn't want it, but I tore open the envelope.

My mother wrote:

> Dear Dorie,
>
> This is a letter from a mother to her daughter. My darling daughter, twenty-three years ago on November 27, 1941, after much pain, I held you in my arms. To me, you were a precious baby, and I loved you and cared for you the best I knew how. The years slipped by, and you grew into a strong, healthy girl for which I was very thankful. I tried to help you see true values and to train you in the way you should go.
>
> *[Oh Mama, I'm so sorry. I don't want to make you sad.]*
>
> I saw you yield your life to Him, and you finished high school and went on to do what was in the plan for you.
>
> *[The plan, Mama? Really? Did God have a plan for Linda?]*
>
> As your mother, I was watching you and praying for you. I saw a girl entering the life of womanhood with a beautiful Christian character. Then, daughter, something began to change. The willingness to yield to the wishes of others first, of being thoughtful of others, was being replaced by a selfish attitude, I heard remarks like, "I don't have to do it if I don't want to. I have a right to do things my way."

[Yes, Mama, I said that. And I still mean it. Yes, and I'll say it again right now. I have the right to do things my way.]

Oh, daughter, my heart aches for you. I can never tell you in words, for you are hurting yourself by resisting.

[The urge to tear the letter into shreds smaller than Leon's took hold of me. Anger served its purpose and kept me from collapsing into tears.]

Oh, my dearest daughter, the Lord sets before each of us life and death. Choose life. Yield yourself to Him, and yield obedience to those over you.

[Mama, I wish I could tell you that obedience to those over me isn't working, but I won't hurt you by arguing.]

Get your eyes on Jesus and follow Him. I am praying for you.

With all my love,
Mother

My world was closing in. I had never made decisions on my own. There was no David. I was over the "I Shall Always Love You." And I was still that girl who said, "I have a right to do things my way." But it was so hard. I didn't know how to do it or what to do.

"Glady," I began when we were alone in the kitchen the next day. "I want to get married.

How do I find a husband?"

Years later, my sister Muriel told me she had used those exact words when she arrived in Connecticut at nineteen. Poor Glady, as if she had a magic ball and husbands would appear.

"You have to get a job," Glady answered, matter-of-factly. That was it. End of discussion.

I went down to my room. How could I tell her I didn't know how to get a job? I had never known a woman with a job other than canvassing or keeping house. Teaching didn't count. I wasn't trained; I was just faking it.

Then it hit me. Glady was telling me I had to work. I couldn't stay for free. I knew she would never send me back, but I was at an impasse. And there was no husband around the corner.

My niece's door was open as I passed it on my way downstairs that night. Her lamp cast a soft glow, and the covers were turned down on her bed. She had been studying, and books were spread across her desk. She must think I'm weird. Or worse, what if she pities me?

If only I could tell someone how afraid I was to be out in the world, away from the safety of my church. I felt sure Glady had gone through this when she left the love and approval of our parents. Just like her, I was dead to them now. In my mother's letter, I could feel it. Over and over, she told me I was wrong, that I was choosing evil, that I must repent to be part of her world.

I approached Glady the next day when the children were at school. "I need to pray with someone," I said. "I think I need to pray with a preacher."

Glady made a phone call and took me to see a preacher later that morning. We knelt to pray in the living room of his house. I said the words I had been taught: "Thy will, not mine." I knew, even as I said them, I wasn't praying for guidance. These were words of surrender. "I have to go back," I said quietly in the car. It wasn't because I chose the church but because I didn't know how to live without it.

Chapter 41
Job Corps

And I did go back—back with my parents, back with the church. I spent the summer of 1966 helping at High Desert Mission in Gallup, New Mexico. The school year had been a repeat of the same old questions about the church compounded by my struggle with the concept of love. The love notes continued from Leon but I had discovered the term *platonic*. I shared it with him, but the distinct feeling prevailed that "love" was a dangerous word to throw around.

I was now sitting in the bed of an old pickup truck on my way from New Mexico to the annual church convention in Potomac. My glance fell on my little blue suitcase stacked with the others in the front of the camper closest to the cab. I had almost lost that suitcase when I handed it to a red cap porter in Chicago before boarding the train for High Desert Mission. I had released the suitcase into the porter's hands while searching in my purse for my ticket. Then I ran to the waiting train, sending a hope and a prayer that my suitcase would go with me. A prickling unease in the back of my mind told me I should've given the porter some money, or at least my name. But I had never used a red cap before, and I didn't have money to spare.

Mrs. Hill, the High Desert Mission director, met me at the train station in Gallup. The look she gave me when I tried to explain my missing suitcase made my shoulders droop and my cheeks burn. "Did it get loaded on the train? Do you have a receipt for it?" She already knew I'd messed up.

"I don't know, and he didn't give me anything." My voice came out squeaky and breathy, like a child's.

"Did you have your name on it?"

"I think so." I was drawing a blank. I couldn't remember if it had a name tag or not. "It was blue," I told her.

"Let me see what I can do." She marched off, leaving me standing outside. I leaned on the green wall of the train depot, swallowing back tears. It was dawning on me that I might have lost my suitcase forever. There was another look when she returned, a cross between sympathy and disbelief that anyone could be so stupid. "They'll try to locate it," she said. "We'll call tomorrow to see if they have it."

Almost all my clothes were in that suitcase, but the thing that crushed my heart was that my black leather Bible with gold-edged pages was in it too—the Bible I had bought with my graduation money. If it were lost, I would never be able to replace it with one so special. They found my suitcase the next day.

Now, I was on my way back to our church convention in Potomac, Illinois. I made sure my suitcase was within arm's reach at all times. We began our trip in the afternoon and would arrive at the church campgrounds the next day. It was going to be a long twenty-four-hour trip. I was sitting on layers of blankets and Indian rugs, which did little to absorb the bumps of the corrugated metal truck floor. Overhead, I inspected the camper shell. I could see daylight where it was attached to the sides of the truck, and air rushed in, threatening to drown out any conversation as we traveled. There was a small window on each side panel, but the wood framing made it impossible to lean our backs against it. A window in the back allowed a view of the sky behind us.

I could see into the cab through another window in front. Mary Alice sat on the passenger side, and her brother, Joe, was driving. Mary Alice was a couple years younger than I and had been my Navajo companion in mission work that summer. We visited families on the reservation, cleaned up around the mission, and spent time hiking and hunting for pieces of ancient pottery and tiny black obsidian arrowheads buried in the desert behind the buildings. Joe owned the truck and served as the mission's main interpreter. He laughed at my attempts to speak his language. "It's the tone," he would say. "Don't say that word. You're cussing."

Across from me in the camper was Esther, their mother, and her husband, Money. I moved my legs when Esther moved hers. Our feet met in the middle, my sturdy brown shoes and nylons sharing space with her scuffed black loafers and white anklets. She grinned at me. She didn't speak English, but her smile communicated pure joy and excitement for the trip. Her gray hair was pulled back in a braid, and her tan face was deeply creased from a lifetime in the desert. She had grown up tending sheep and now used their wool to weave beautiful rugs and saddle blankets. She occasionally leaned over to Money, their voices rising and falling in staccato tones, punctuated by the rumble of the truck and the whistling wind through the camper shell.

We had been traveling for a few hours when Esther unfolded a white towel on her lap. She passed me a pancake-sized piece of fry bread with puffy bubbles where the air had been captured in the hot cooking grease. With her biggest smile, she brought out another towel full of sheep ribs cooked over a slow fire. We sat savoring the ribs and tearing our bread, nodding and smiling.

I watched as the last rays of the setting sun slid through the back window of the camper. Darkness descended quickly, lit occasionally by the headlights of passing cars. In my half-sleep, my mind wandered to my latest dream, my new plan. Did I dare hope once again that I could find my way out, that I could become an independent person, make my own decisions, earn my own money, and escape?

During the summer in New Mexico, Mary Alice had spoken confidently about what she planned to do next in her life. She and Joe had a brother living in Chicago who told her about a new program where she could be trained as a nurse's aide, free of cost. "Can anyone get this training?" I asked.

"Yes," Mary Alice told me after checking with her brother. "If you don't have any money and want a job, you can apply." Suddenly, becoming a nurse's aide became the most wonderful job in the world.

"Can I go with you to apply?" I asked. We talked about what the job entailed. "It sounds like an aide helps nurses. When Linda was in the hospital, nurses took care of her. I'd be good at making beds and emptying bedpans." Mary Alice laughed.

Somehow, I would make it happen. I dreamed of that job all through the summer and throughout the night in the back of the truck. High Desert Mission operated independently from our church, so Mary Alice could choose the training she wanted, but I had to ask. I was supposed to teach again, and part of me worried about my wild new plan. My life had always been about following orders, going to High Desert, returning for another year at the school, and forever dropping into and out of the roles the church told me to play. As long as I obeyed, I was safe from hellfire, and my parents would love me. Leon, the most powerful man in the church, was my friend. But was that enough? My heart told me I was missing out. There had to be more.

Before the convention ended, I presented my case to Leon. "It's a hospital job, and the training is free," I told him. "I watched

Linda suffer in the hospital, and taking care of patients will let me do something in her memory."

He couldn't deny that, could he? Just to be sure, I added, "If Mary Alice can get a job, I should be able to get one too. How could it be God's will for her but not for me?" In my most forceful voice I added, "And it's free."

After the convention, I went with Mary Alice and the canvassing ladies to Race Street in Chicago. Helen, the crew manager, set up beds for us in the basement, and all I had to do was wait until Monday morning to apply for my free training. My sleep was sweet with promise.

The Job Corps had been created two years previously and served underprivileged young people ages sixteen to twenty-four. I didn't know I was pushing the upper limits. The office was in the basement of a government building in downtown Chicago. They called Mary Alice first. When I walked down the hall a few minutes later, panic fought with my hope. I had never had an interview. How would I do? "I am twenty-four," I said, sitting on the edge of my seat, facing the director. "Yes, I graduated from high school." She wouldn't know it was a tiny religious school in the cornfields.

"What was your last job?" I had never had a job, how could I explain that?

"I've been working for the church." She strained to hear the words I whispered. Was I imagining her stare? No, I had seen that look before. It conveyed crazy, lazy or dumb. I filled out the sheet titled Health Record and then stepped on the scale. The woman recorded my weight and went around to sit at her desk. I stood. For a moment she studied my record. She was frowning when she looked up again.

"You are five pounds overweight," she said. "Our cutoff is 140 pounds for your height." I was five foot seven. I wasn't skinny but I wasn't fat either. How could I be overweight?

"If I lose five pounds, can I come back, and will I be accepted?" I knew I sounded desperate.

She nodded. "It might be harder to lose weight than you think, but you can come back." My shoulders drooped as I turned and walked out of the room.

Mary Alice was waiting. I could see by her happy smile and dancing eyes that she had been accepted. "I have to come back," I told her, my voice cracking.

I didn't go back. I couldn't stay in Chicago until I lost five pounds. I would soon be teaching again.

Chapter 42
Next New Plan

I was back teaching again at the school for 1966–67, and I was once more the church secretary for Leon. My typing had improved, but my outlook had not. My attempts at freedom had fizzled out one by one. Finally, one day when most of the leaves had blown off the trees and the clouds outside matched my mood, I turned to Leon.

"How can I get training to be a nurse?"

I learned that day that colleges taught nursing. I knew that college was not an option in our church. Leon had not attended college nor had any of my high school or post-high school teachers. But he had sent me to a class at the teachers' college when I was in Union Grove. Now he told me there was a test to get into college called the SAT. Taking this test was beyond my wildest dreams, but when I asked if I could try it, Leon shrugged and told me to go for it.

I bought a book on how to prepare for the SAT. There were two parts: math and English. The math problems were the kind I loved in my chemistry and physics books. I was also comfortable with the English section. With Miss Hey, my English teacher in high school, we had diagrammed Bible verses that covered the entire blackboard. We also studied the Word Power lists from *Reader's Digest*. I took the test, but as winter dragged on, I filed college into the wastebasket of lost dreams.

Then Leon told me in March that my test results were in and the counselor at the high school wanted me to come to his office. Even if I passed the test, I knew there was no way I could pay for college. I walked slowly down the hall of Potomac High School and sat down facing the counselor's desk.

"So you are the one with those scores," he greeted and handed me a booklet. "If you'll look at the ratings, you placed at the 99th percentile in English and the 98th in math. You could go to Harvard with those scores."

"Oh, no!" I cut him off. Harvard sounded too much like hell. "I want to be a nurse."

I applied to several private colleges in Illinois with four-year nursing programs and was offered scholarships from all of them. The best fit was North Park, run by the Swedish Covenant Church in Chicago. I could retain my connection with the canvassing ladies of the church, and the train would provide transportation home on weekends. My scholarship paid the tuition, and a state grant picked up the rest. My life was moving forward. My heart soared.

One day later that spring when my steps were bouncing high, Leon stopped me. "Have you thought of becoming a missionary nurse?"

No, no, I had not. I wanted to shut that thought down. I simply shook my head. In my shrouded dreams, I was hoping to find my way out into a world where I could be me, where I could find the man who was waiting for me. If only I had a chance.

That night I remembered that on one of my trips to Mexico, I had seen a five-year-old girl with her fingers webbed and the skin on her arm drawn tight with burn scars. I had seen children born with defects like Linda who never received help. Was I called to help them? I had never forgotten an occasion when I was about ten years old in Sunday school in Milwaukee. My father was standing beside the piano.

"Daddy, I am going to be a missionary when I grow up," I looked up at him.

My father looked at me with a half-smile and then gazed away into the distance as if he had not heard me. He said nothing. I guessed I said the wrong thing or he would have been happy. Maybe I was not good enough. Missionaries in our church were saved and sanctified, and I didn't even understand sanctification.

As I knelt by my bed that night after teaching school, my mind returned to Leon's question. I had copied the old hymn "The Missionary's Call" by Nathan Brown into my Bible, and I turned to it.

> My soul is not at rest.
> There comes a strange and secret whisper to my spirit,
> Like a dream of night,
> That tells me I am on enchanted ground.
> Why live I here?
> The vows of God are on me, and I may not stop to
>   play with shadows, or pluck earthly flowers,
> Till I my work have done, and rendered up account.
> And I will go.
> I may no longer doubt to give up friends and idle hopes,
> And every tie that binds my heart to thee, my country.

I had memorized those words, and my heart responded. Yes, I would become a missionary nurse. I wasn't sure I was saved and sanctified. Well, I was sure I was not sanctified, but Leon thought I should be a missionary nurse. Yes, this was my destiny.

Chapter 43
Betrayal

When school ended that spring, I went to Brownsville, Texas, with Leon's family. They made this trip for Vacation Bible School and special meetings each summer, and I had helped before. I was thinking of my future career as a missionary nurse. I was answering my call.

It was the last Saturday night of special meetings before the Grahams returned to Illinois. I would remain for a few more weeks. We had been in Matamoros, Mexico, at one of the convert's homes. Leon's wife and children had stayed home that night, and after the service, I was the only one in the car, sitting in the passenger seat where Leon's wife usually sat. Leon turned the car onto the Padre Island Beach road on the US side. I looked at him, but neither of us spoke.

When we reached the beach, he drove along the wet sand. It was dark, and the beach was deserted. Moonlight skipped in a rippling path over the water toward the horizon, and foamy white waves crept up the shore. We got out and began walking. The air between us was charged. I was overwhelmed that he would bring me here to share the beauty of the night.

Then it happened. He was holding me, kissing me on the lips. "No tongues," he whispered, pressing his lips harder into mine.

It was my first kiss, and whatever "tongues" meant, I did not know or care. When the kiss ended, his arms remained around me.

"I just can't let you go," he whispered. He kissed me again.

He loves me. He truly loves me. My heart was bursting. All those notes about loving me forever were true. My world as I knew it ceased to exist, and I nestled closer to him, my arms tightening around his neck. We kissed again, the pounding of our hearts drowning out the rolling tide. When we got back into the car, there was silence. Neither of us spoke on the trip back.

The romantic feeling was already fading when he pulled up to the curb beside the church. Before I could move, he grabbed the side of my neck and pushed my head down onto his lap, wedging it under the steering wheel. I had no clue that it might be a sexual position. I stayed in that uncomfortable spot, the steering wheel pressing into the back of my head for what felt like an eternity, though it was probably only minutes. When I tried to sit up, he forced me back down.

Whatever beauty I had felt on the beach vanished. Guilt and shame surged through me. And I did not try to move again. All I could think of was his wife—her trust and her place beside him in that car. Something sacred had been broken by that kiss and completely obliterated by the pressure of his hand still holding my head down.

He had crossed a line, and I was numb, powerless to stop him. I didn't yet know that the church itself had cracked open that night, though it would stagger on for another ten years in its death throes. But I knew this much: I would never be the same again.

As I walked the two blocks to the missionaries' house where I was staying, I trembled. My whole body was shaking. I would not learn about pastoral abuse for another thirty years. At the time, all I knew was that he was my trusted counselor, my spiritual guide, the leader of our church, and he had let me down. What did that mean?

I was no child, but I was still a little girl in so many ways—sheltered, ignorant, unprepared to stand against a man with nineteen more years of experience and power over not just me but everyone I loved. In that car, with my head forced onto his lap, he had crushed what was left of my innocence.

I would bury the kiss. I would bury the walk on the beach. I would bury the betrayal so deep in the folds of memory that it would become almost dreamlike, easier to forget than to examine. It was easier to pretend it had never happened at all.

I returned to Mount Moriah in July for Girls' Camp. Our church invited the children from the Sunday schools, and the canvassers earned stars in their heavenly crowns if the children found Jesus at the camp. This was my happy time, one week when I could be who I was born to be. I loved to swim in the muddy river, wander the woodland paths, make up funny skits for the campfire, and finally—with the setting sun and flames leaping into the night sky—bask in the love and presence of God.

Most of all, I treasured my assignment as counselor to the youngest girls—bubbly, giggling nine-year-olds who were too young to plan mischief but old enough for big excitement. I loved the one night my girls and I slept in the tent in the woods. When one of them went inside with me to deposit our blankets, a snake was sleeping on the floor of the tent. That night, every rustle of leaves turned into a monster.

I had read books about edible woodland plants, roots, and survival skills in the wild. If a flat rock were heated in the campfire, it could become hot enough to fry an egg. I thought it would be a great idea to cook our eggs in the morning campfire. We went down to the river and gathered flat rocks to fry our eggs. We washed them and placed them in the fire pit the night before. While the rocks were heating the next morning, I helped the girls wrap biscuit dough around their sticks to cook over the fire.

Before we could crack our eggs, a piece of rock flew out of the fire. Then another missile, and another. I screamed for the girls to get back and led them quickly away from the fire to the dining room. When I got a break, I went back to my survival book.

"Do not use rocks that are wet or have been in water," I read. "Rocks from a river can become dangerous because water may be trapped in the cracks."

We would never have rocks for breakfast again. I winced at my mistake, not dreaming that the snake in the tent and the flying missiles were omens of what was to come.

All of Leon's charisma and charm were on display at the campfire on the last night of camp. The girls' faces glowed with excitement and expectation as his stories waxed eloquent. When he tossed the last piece of wood on the fire, the flames burned brightly, and sparks exploded into the star-studded sky. My heart was one with the aura of the Higher Power around us, and I hugged the little girls sitting next to me on the log.

As my little girls prepared for bed, a song was running through my head. I sat on the side of my cot, softly singing until the room grew still and the music of the crickets took over.

> Someone's singing, Lord, kumbaya.
> Someone's singing, Lord, kumbaya.
> Someone's singing, Lord, kumbaya.
> O Lord, kumbaya.

I was still awake when the door opened quietly behind me at the head of my bed. I sat up, turning sharply. It was Leon. He knelt on the cement floor beside my cot and pushed my shoulder down into the pillow. I grabbed the sheet to cover my shortie pajamas and strained my ears for the soft breathing of my nine-year-olds. I tried to sit up to make sure none of them had awakened, but the pressure of his hand against my shoulder bore down, and I fell back.

I clutched the sheet under my chin as his hand left my shoulder, slipped beneath the sheet, and found my thigh. I held my breath. I tried to shift position, but he held me down. When he finally stood and left the room, my brain refused to think. He could do whatever he wanted with me, and I would not utter a word. My whole world would collapse if I told, and there would be no more camp. The canvasssers' lifeline would be severed. And all my parents' and sister's sacrifices would be in vain. I dropped into a dark place. No one would believe me. Eventually, the exhaustion of the day overtook me, and I slept.

The next morning, my girls dressed as usual, their high little voices floating on the rays of sunlight filling the room. At breakfast, Leon thanked God for our food. He laughed and chatted. I stared at his middle finger.

Chapter 44
Fasting and Praying

A month later I sat in the back seat with two of the aging canvassers as we traveled from Chicago to Mount Moriah for the church convention at the end of the summer, just before I would leave for college. It was the only vacation the members of the church were allowed, and the mood in the car was filled with happy anticipation of visiting with friends again. I had canvassed with them since camp, earning a little money for myself too. Only Helen, the crew manager, knew I was working for money for new clothes for college.

"Keep quiet about why you are there," Leon had told me after camp. He recognized my need for new clothes for college before I did. My clothes were long past their expiration date, but all church workers were equally poor. Our slips and bras were held together with safety pins and prayers. Our shoes were worn until the holes in the soles let in so much water that water puddled inside. The style of our dresses never changed: gray uniforms and practical skirts well below the knees.

I had $50 in my purse, more money than any of the other women would ever have to spend on themselves. Soon I would be poring over the Sears Roebuck catalog with my mother to pick out my new clothes for college. It was like getting ready for high school, only this time I had my own money, and I could not wait for the freedom I would soon enjoy.

My room in the old folks' home was across from the kitchen. For the convention, my mother gave Leon a vacant room next to mine. He preached every night. My brother-in-law Ed and Miss Hey rotated preaching in the afternoons. Leon's sermons were the highlight, the bright spot, the inspiration to renew consecration and devotion for another year of self-sacrifice for the church.

One afternoon as I was returning to my room, Leon stopped me. "Come by my room," he said in my ear.

I had been giving him a wide berth, with my thoughts flitting between excitement for college and dedicating my life to God for missionary work. However, my mind kept reverting to the times he touched me. Did he really like me that way? It had to be wrong, but he was the church. Did he know something I didn't know about sexual behavior?

Leon stepped up as he answered my knock. I felt a fizzling energy between us as he leaned closer. "This must be why people dance," I whispered. He smiled.

"I'm going to be in the woods fasting and praying for the service tonight," he said as I backed into the hall. "You can come to pray with me if you want."

I had prayed with him so often over the years that it was easy to take it at face value. And I wanted to see him, to understand the powerful attraction that came over me when we were close.

After the supper bell rang and the grounds were empty, I ran down the road to the pasture beside the woods. The afternoon sun was beginning to dip over the trees along the river. The pasture belonged to a nearby farmer, but there were no cows. This was my happy place. Two large apple trees stood in the middle, loaded with big, perfect apples.

Unlike the orchard back at the school with small, misshapen apples with wormholes, these apples retained their perfect shape, even the apples that fell to the ground. I picked a large red apple and one from the tree with yellow apples. As I approached the woods, a deer jumped over the fence in front of me. I stopped and watched it bound away before crawling through a broken part of the wire.

I found Leon near the trail, kneeling next to a fallen tree with his Bible propped open. After giving him the apples, I selected a place at the other end of the log. I prayed first, asking for the message to speak to my heart. My anxiety was palpable as I prayed for guidance for the big changes coming to my life. I wanted to believe that his strange display of attention was born out of concern as I stepped out into the world.

On the way back to the campgrounds, I stopped again at the apple trees. Munching on the crisp, sweet fruit, I felt gratitude for the mentor who helped keep my vision clear and my goal steadfast in order to fulfill God's plan in my life. With his help I had found purpose to live again after Linda.

Leon's sermon that night resonated with my soul. I looked out over the women seated around me, graying hair bound tightly at the backs of their necks, handkerchiefs in their hands. The gathering was smaller than it had been in previous years. There were a few married couples now. Only single men and women had filled the seats before. The young people had dwindled as one by one they had left the church after high school.

My thoughts strayed as I glanced over to the men's side. I could see no life partner for me there. But these were my people. The safety and belonging far outweighed thoughts of leaving.

This family was not only my parents and my sister Gloria but all the brothers and sisters in God worshiping with me that night. I would remain true to them in college.

Chapter 45
Starting College

I carried my blue suitcase into the freshmen girls' college dorm on move-in day. North Park College was in the heart of a busy northside Chicago neighborhood with the Chicago River running through the campus. This would be my home for the next four years.

I found my private room on the second floor and closed the door. The sunlight from the small, west-facing window was blocked by the building just behind it, and I flipped on the light switch. The sounds outside my door were plainly audible—chatter, shouting, and laughter. And I was hearing music, worldly music. How would I ever adjust to rock and roll? And what about teenage girls with every hairstyle except a braid. And what about their shorts and jeans? The brown walls of my little room closed in.

The first crisis of my education was not evolution in biology or principles of religion in philosophy. The little book *Utopia* by Thomas More was required reading for Honors English 101. On the first day of class, I couldn't believe what I was hearing. *Utopia* was a new word for me, and as the professor questioned the class on its meaning, I sat in shock. Was there really a name for an alternative society where people had everything in common, where everyone shared possessions and were governed by a moral code? This was like the Bible School.

I waited after class and approached the teacher's desk. She looked up and listened as I tried to find the words. "I think I grew up in a group that practiced this kind of living."

She smiled. "I had another student who also came from a closed society. It will be interesting to hear your story."

I returned to my little dorm room and threw my books on the bed. That afternoon I read straight through *Utopia*. After I closed it, I sat thinking. I shouldn't have talked to the teacher. I didn't grow up in a utopia. I heard the part about sharing possessions and a closed society and got it all wrong.

My "utopia" had been Mr. Hitchcock's cottage on Lake Pewaukee and the strawberries and cream on his dining room table. It was my father who believed in sharing all things, certainly the two houses he had owned and given to the church. But my family had not lived in harmony. Half of my siblings had been cut off and lost to the world. I knew I was not going to share my story. Whatever kind of group I was raised in, my view of the world was warped, and it was not a utopia.

Chapter 46
Weekends

One thing would save me and provide a touch of normalcy in my life as I considered the giant chasm between my normal and the normal around me. I planned to go to the church home for canvassers on Race Avenue every Saturday night. It wasn't that I loved canvassing homes, but I was studying to become a missionary nurse for the church. And Leon would be there preaching every Sunday. For years he had been making the trip from Potomac to Race Street every Saturday afternoon. He would sleep over and preach in the church in the alley on Sunday morning. It was vital to keep up the spirits of the women canvassers since their financial support was keeping the church going and providing income for Leon's family, as well.

I sat waiting in the dorm lobby that first Saturday afternoon. Eventually, I would learn to use public transportation, but Leon was coming for me that day. My heart raced when I saw him. I sat in his car near the door in the front seat. His black felt hat that covered his bald head lay between us.

We had hardly left campus when he reached for my hand. He pulled me over, placing my hand on his pants. All my inhibitions and religious taboos faded; right and wrong smoldered and turned to ashes. I was with the man who loved me. He knew I needed him. He knew I was lonely and bewildered in my new life. And on the beach he had told me he needed me as much as I needed him. This was a game I was willing to play and powerless to stop. I closed the space between us, crushing his hat, oblivious to the Saturday night Chicago traffic.

That night, I went to the basement where Helen had given Mary Alice and me beds a year before. Hers was untouched under a small cellar window that caught the light from occasional passing cars. Toward the back, I found my spot, pitch black except for the faint glow from the stairwell. I was thinking about Leon when I heard the stairs creak. It was not Mary Alice.

The next morning at breakfast, I sat beside Auntie Hannah. At the other end of the table, Leon prayed for the food and for the hands that prepared it and then chatted amiably with the women. Auntie Hannah had prepared that food, just as she had fed him years ago in Union Grove when I was eight. Back then, she called him "God's precious young man." This morning was my first taste of the dissonance I would battle throughout my college years. Leon had snuck down the stairs last night to see me—Auntie Hannah's stairs.

The church in an alley was made up of three cramped rooms. The largest had two high windows and a door that opened to the street. The back rooms were small and dark, meant for Sunday school classes for the neighborhood children, but Leon and I met there. We were using the same space where innocent little hands colored Bible pictures and children learned Scripture verses. I hated the lie we lived, the trust we violated. The women around us believed in his holiness. And I played my part in the illusion.

Week after week, our pattern became fixed. I would meet him on Saturday, but every Sunday afternoon, I returned to my dark little dorm room and cried. This was not how I thought love should be, meeting and leaving, repeated over and over forever. My tears were not only for me but for the women of Race Street, for my parents, for Gloria, and for Leon's family.

One Saturday evening, Leon and I drove downtown. Seeing an open parking spot beside Buckingham Fountain, he pulled in. It was late fall. The fountain was still illuminated, water cascading in arches against the silhouetted skyline. We were acting like out-of-control teenagers when I saw the flashing blue lights outside the car. A policeman tapped on the window. I muffled a scream. What would my parents say if we were arrested? Leon zipped up and stepped out of the car. I forced back tears and waited. When he finally returned, he turned to me and said, "They always get the man because he can't hide it." That was all he said. We drove back to Race Street in silence. I was still trembling when I got out of the car. What story had he told the policeman, and what did that make me? I never asked.

That Sunday afternoon, I took the bus back to school. I walked past the park along the Chicago River and then turned to sit on a bench. I didn't want to return to my solitary room to face the torrent of tears that would follow. I looked out at the college students lazing on the grass beside the river. The scene highlighted the contrast between my life and theirs. Eventually, I returned to my dorm room, mourning the life I had and the one I could not have.

There were thirty-three girls, including me, enrolled in the four-year nursing program. In my sophomore year, we moved into the nurses' dorm across from Swedish Covenant Hospital, which was affiliated with North Park College. A few girls who were majoring in other subject, also moved in. My roommate was a history major, as serious about her studies as I was about mine. When we were in our room at the same time, we were deep into our books. I welcomed the silence, the structure, the sense of purpose. It felt like a world I could depend on, but I was still absent from my dorm room on Saturday nights. I buried my secrets deep, but the conflict between truth and deceit never left me. I told myself it was the part of my life that had become inescapable but that it would end when I became a missionary nurse. Someday, I would walk away into God's Plan and leave my deep inner dissonance behind.

We were noisy with excitement the night of the nursing students' capping ceremony that took place after two years of nursing training. It was also the night I gave up on the sacred tenet of long hair. I blinked back tears of frustration as I tried to pin my cap over the bun on my head. The starched white hat tilted like a bird taking flight, no matter how many bobby pins I used. But I had reached my first goal. I was now a nurse in my blue and white uniform who was looking forward to two more years crammed with training in hospitals around the city. Four-year nurses were destined for leadership positions, a future I almost believed was the Plan, but the vision was becoming hazy. I began to wear my hair free at shoulder length.

Chapter 47
Flat Tire

"I've arranged a summer of missionary work for you in Mexico," Leon told me one spring evening at the end of my sophomore year in the nursing program.

"You'll be helping Lorry Smith who runs the Metropolitan Church mission in Brownsville, Texas, and then you'll go with our church to Mexico for Vacation Bible School."

Metropolitan Church? That was the Bible School. Did they still have missionaries? Did my parents know I would be working for them, and did they care? But what did I know? When Leon spoke, I listened. I followed orders.

Vicky, who was seventeen, was also helping with the summer program. I remembered her father and aunt from the Bible School. We sat together in the back of the Travelall, a boxy utility vehicle packed with supplies for a month in Mexico. Our driver, Lorry Smith, was a middle-aged woman with the same plain hair and clothes as all the women in our church.

Our destination was the home of a Mexican pastor in Saltillo. I wasn't expecting the large white house surrounded by a high wall on a tree-lined street where we stayed the first week. Clearly, the Metropolitan Church had more resources for missionaries than our church. Lorry preached in the evenings for the Mexican pastor, and after a week of Vacation Bible School, we set out for villages farther south.

We had been traveling over dry, unpaved desert roads all afternoon when a monsoon thunderstorm unleashed a torrent of blinding rain. We stopped and waited for it to end. When we drove on, the road suddenly ended. There was no bridge, just an angry, swirling river of brown water.

"I remember this wash," Lorry said. "It's not deep. This is just runoff from the storm." She gripped the steering wheel and drove into the water. The vehicle swayed as the current pushed us sideways. I caught my breath and grabbed for the boxes that were sliding around. The engine stalled, and the tires crashed on large rocks beneath the surface. We sat there baking in the hot sun while Lorry tried again and again to start the engine.

"I guess I'll have to go for help," Lorry said. "You girls stay here and take care of things."

This wasn't the kind of adventure we'd bargained for, but Vicky and I giggled at the story we'd have to tell.

Eventually, we heard the chugging of a tractor. Lorry had returned with several men. As they waded into the water to attach chains, I could hear them talking. It was clear what they thought of the foolish American woman who had driven into a wash during monsoon season. What I had assumed was a simple blunder was, in fact, a life-threatening mistake.

Vicky and I waded through the water, carrying our shoes. The men laughed and cheered as they pulled the car over the rocks with the tractor, slowly dragging it to safety.

The scenery began to change as we drove into the foothills of the mountains. Wind- twisted trees were scattered between rocky outcrops. We climbed higher. The village where we would hold our next Vacation Bible School was nestled in a valley. Adobe houses on one side opened directly onto the street. On the other side, a stream splashed over the rocks.

We drove farther up the mountain and stopped beside a small white church with a wooden cross nailed to the door. The sun was already setting behind the mountains, crimson and gold streaks telling the day goodnight. When we had unloaded the last of the boxes, we made our beds on the floor.

The next morning, the children began arriving for Vacation Bible School before we finished tidying up. They stayed until we sent them home each day. I loved the work, but the question nagged at me: Why was I working with the Metropolitan Church Mission? I turned it over and over in my mind. When I became a missionary nurse, would I be serving here for the Metropolitan Church?

That evening, Lorry told us about the tire the rocks had ripped up. I didn't give it much thought. Surely she had a spare. But the spare was old, and just an hour after the men aired it up with a hand pump, it began to go flat again.

"We need a new tire," Lorry said, "but we'll have to drive all the way back to the city, and that'll delay the work."

Lorry managed to find someone to patch the spare before we left for the next village, and we played "patch the tire" for the next two weeks. Sometimes it would hold for a day and we'd thank God for traveling mercies. Other times, it would be flat again before we could drive away.

We had been staying in churches, but in the last village we were invited into a family's home. They had small children, and the mother insisted we eat with them. The father worked on an avocado farm. Every meal, we ate avocados with corn tortillas and avocados with beans. A few scrawny chickens wandered in and out of the house.

On our final evening, they served us a celebratory meal of *pollo y arroz*, chicken and rice. We would be returning to the United States the next day where we could have all the chicken we wanted. Why had we eaten one of theirs? The Bible claims, "It is more blessed to give than to receive" (Acts 20:35), but it didn't seem right to me. I began to wonder if our message of heavenly riches was truly worth their generous gifts to us here and now.

We started back to the United States the next morning with our patched tire. After only a few miles, we were scraping along, and the tire was flat again. Vicky's parents were waiting for her in Brownsville, and I was expected back that night at our church missionary home. Up ahead, we saw a group of people waiting by the side of the road. Lorry walked over to them.

"A truck will be along to take you to the border," she told us when she returned. "Walk from there to the mission. I'll hitch a ride back to the village and wait for a new tire."

She left us to climb into the back of an old farm truck with rough wooden slats along the sides. We were packed in, lurching along as the hot, dry air snatched away our conversation.

People got off; others got on. When a woman climbed in carrying a tiny baby, everyone made room for her behind the cab, out of the wind. "The baby has diarrhea," she told me. "He won't nurse. He's going to die if I don't reach a doctor soon."

I decided then that this was where I would serve and use my nurse's training. It was definitely needed whether the rest of my message was vital or not.

The following Monday, I met up with Martha, a single missionary from our church. She was passionately committed to her calling. We walked across the border together, back into Mexico, carrying our suitcases, and boarded a bus. It was crowded, and our bags were tossed on top of the bus with piles of fruit, potatoes, bicycles, and crates of chickens.

When we reached Ciudad Victoria around noon, Pastor Felix was waiting with his burro, unbothered by the crowds and traffic. When our suitcases were finally thrown down, Felix tied them to the saddle, one on each side. I trudged along while Felix and Martha talked. We climbed up the mountain for a couple of hours, the sun at our backs. The village lay stretched across a flat plateau surrounded by hills.

We slept on the church floor again. The next morning, Felix's wife brewed coffee while the women and girls carried water jugs from the well in the center of the village, balancing the jugs over their shoulders on a stick. The children stayed with us all day, happy, noisy, and full of life.

One evening, when the church was quiet, Martha and I shared a can of corned beef we had brought with us. The next morning, a dog ran around with the empty can in its mouth. I felt embarrassed, as if that can of meat should have been given to Felix and his family who struggled with food shortages. Again, I wondered if what we were offering was enough. In a week, we would return to our comfortable world. Martha and Lorry seemed fulfilled by this life. Why did I feel like an impostor? Why did I doubt the value of the message I carried?

Maybe it was because I felt unworthy.

We walked back down the mountain on July 19, 1969, at the end of Vacation Bible School, our suitcases tied once again to the burro. I stared up at the bright blue sky. I would soon be back across the border. The news would be whether *Apollo 11* and its astronauts had landed on the moon. But it was so hot, and I was so tired. All I really wished for that day was that I could ride that burro. I stumbled along behind it.

At the end of August, I was back at Mount Moriah for the church convention. When I walked into the Sunday night preaching service in my new black dress with a white inset down the front, Leon told me later that he caught his breath and lost his train of thought.

I sat staring at the aging canvassers in the seats in front of me as they leaned into every word Leon spoke. My gaze stopped on Martha with her grey hair in a tidy bun, a dedicated missionary, gladly sacrificing her life on the mission field. These women were the epitome of what I was supposed to become. Continuing on my chosen path, the Plan spelled the end of my dreams to be married and have children. That night, my vision of becoming a missionary nurse shriveled. I was so close to committing, but I could not.

Chapter 48
Career Change

I returned to college that fall, a week before classes began. First on my agenda Monday morning was a visit to my academic advisor. "Would it be possible for me to switch from nursing and get my degree in science education?"

Just like that, my career was rerouted. There would be no missionary nurse. Our church high school had begun a new phase since I had taught there two years ago. The name was changed to become more interdenominational, and the goal was Christian education with less stringent rules. The number of students had doubled, and the old school at the farm had become too small. My parents and the old people were moved to the farm, and the Mount Moriah campgrounds became the new school.

I would not leave the church or God, I told myself. I was just giving myself a little more time to hold on to my dreams. That evening, I walked from my dorm through the tunnel under the street to the hospital cafeteria for dinner. I wanted to move out of the nurses' dorm, but I wondered if I could rent a room off campus. The next morning, I headed back to campus to the Student Accounts Office.

"Would I be able to use my financial aid for a room off campus?" I asked.

That afternoon, I began to survey the neighborhood. The streets were lined with Chicago bungalows, sturdy brown brick with arched doorways and windows, some with small covered porches. I walked up and down the streets, knocking on every door. Finally, near the end of a block close to campus, someone pointed across the street. "The lady over there used to rent a room, but I haven't seen anyone recently," the woman said.

I ran across the street and knocked on the door. A little old lady with short grey hair opened it. She looked conservative and reserved. I could see her shrinking back. I gave her my brightest smile. "I am quiet. I have the funds to pay, and I will not bring anyone into your house," I begged.

I held my breath as Ruth invited me in to show me the room at the top of the stairs. It was a small space with a slanted ceiling and a tiny closet. A window facing the street let in the hot afternoon sun. The only furniture was a double bed. I would share the kitchen and bathroom. Ruth was a single lady who had inherited her home from her Swedish immigrant parents and had worked all her life as a secretary in downtown Chicago. I rented the room.

Later that day, I walked 3 miles to a used furniture store and picked out a little table with spindly legs and a straight chair. The plastic seat cushion had seen better days with a pattern carved into it by a knife. The total for both was only $7. I arranged for them to be delivered, and on the way out, I spied a window fan—another bargain. I happily carried it back to my room and set it in the window. It blew hot air around the room all night, but in the morning, it was burned out. I didn't replace it.

On Saturday afternoon, I walked back to the nurses' dorm and waited for Leon to come. "I'm going to be a teacher," I blurted out as soon as I got into the car.

There was silence.

"You know I was interested in nursing because that was the job I wanted with Mary Alice when I had no other choice. I really want to be a biology teacher, and I have enough science credits from nursing to still graduate in two years. Our school needs a science teacher." The silence behind the steering wheel deepened.

Finally, he spoke. "That $500 I arranged for you, for books and other expenses, the donor gave that as a tax deduction for missions."

So that would be the issue he would use to dissuade me. "I won't need it now," I assured him. "I've rented a room off campus, and my rent is less than my dorm housing." Defiance crept into my voice. "Besides, I can get a job as a nurse's aide now at the hospital to help with expenses."

The reality I had repressed came into focus with striking clarity. He had planned to lose me in Mexico. That was his road out of our liaison all along. He would walk away, and I would be a missionary in a foreign land, destined to grow old alone in poverty and self-sacrifice.

There was no fooling around that night.

Chapter 49
The Big Mistake

Two years later, I stood in my black cap and gown, swept along with the excited crowd outside the auditorium on my college graduation afternoon. Scanning for my parents, I spotted my mother first, her radiant smile pulling me toward the small group of my parents, Gloria, Ed, and Leon. Leon's presence required no explanation; he'd offered to drive them. My mother beamed all afternoon, living her deferred dreams through me. I'd grown up hearing how she'd longed to attend high school but couldn't when boarding proved too costly for her parents. She'd felt her mission fulfilled when all her children earned high school diplomas, but college? That lay beyond our family's wildest imaginings.

As I hugged my mother, someone tapped my arm and pressed a handful of gold cords into my palm.

"What am I supposed to do with these?"

"Wear them around your neck," my sister Gloria declared. She shook them out and looped them over my shoulders. How did she know? Later, receiving my diploma, I spotted a few others with gold cords, and I noticed that her placement was correct.

My parents pored over my diploma after the ceremony. "*Summa cum laude*!" they exclaimed. I had never heard the term.

Nearby, a girl from my science classes stood wearing three cords like mine.

"I'm starting at Abbott Laboratories next month," I heard her tell her friends. "I already have the job."

Was that possible? What had I missed? Abbott developed medicines. Could women like me really land such a job? I had been questioning God's plan, but I surmised I had messed up Leon's plan more than God's when I switched majors. My small world trembled that afternoon when I heard there might have been a different way out.

As my graduation gift, my parents had planned to give me a trip to California. My sister Muriel and my brother Floydie had left Connecticut and moved to Los Angeles for work. Though they'd attended Linda's funeral years prior, I knew nothing of their lives or families. While I was in college, my parents had quietly reconnected with their long-exiled children. My mother had finally convinced my father to admit his mistakes and seek forgiveness. Each child and their family had accepted my parents' apologies. Their children were now teenagers or adults, and the magical early years with them had been lost forever. My parents hoped this trip would help all of us reconnect as a family.

Saving for the California trip was no small feat for my parents. They had little income at Mount Moriah working a rundown farm and peddling eggs every Saturday to support the old folks' home and themselves. Any savings they could tuck away meant real sacrifice.

We arrived in California—amazed by my siblings' modern ranch-style houses. Floydie's backyard had an in-ground pool—luxury beyond my wildest dreams. Muriel laughed as she showed our mother her new plush blue parlor chairs. "I always wanted blue," she said.

My siblings' lives overwhelmed me. We attended Floydie's church on Sunday and spent another day at Disneyland with Muriel's family. As "It's a Small World" played, I glanced at my mother smiling beside me in the moving car. Linda and I had often craned our necks passing Kiddieland on the way to church in Milwaukee, yearning for a merry-go-round ride we knew was "worldly." Now we were dining in restaurants with white tablecloths and leather menus. I watched my parents savor it all while my throat tightened.

Muriel and Floydie's wife, my sister-in-law, were comfortable with short curls, slacks, and open-toed shoes. I obsessed over my frumpiness, inexperienced with shopping or style. Even if I left the church now, the gap felt unbridgeable. Their lives existed across a chasm impossible for me to cross. I could never be part of their world.

We were exhausted on the drive home. Silence settled in until I finally spoke. "Floydie's church believes differently than we do," I ventured. "What do you think of a salvation that stays in place even if you commit sins? Daddy, we would've been better off believing that than losing grace every time we lost our tempers."

My mother shifted uncomfortably, but I pressed on. "What if our church got it wrong? What if Floydie's church has it right? You don't truly believe Muriel and Floydie are hell-bound, do you?"

My mother was upset. My father stayed silent. Part of me ached to unburden myself. There was so much more I longed to reveal. Their trust was placed in a sinking ship. No one knew it except me—and Leon. My father, raised in the Metropolitan Church Bible School, cared nothing about other versions of the Protestant religion. I didn't know enough to debate theologies. I had only learned about the doctrine of salvation that could not be undone after visiting my sister Glady in Connecticut. My parents clung to the version of God's Word they had been taught, despite its flaws. It was a pipe dream that they would ever denounce their church. I wanted to tear down all the facade that propped us up, but I couldn't.

That summer I moved into the basement of the girls' dorm at Mount Moriah. My room was where my father once washed and packaged his Saturday eggs. A single wooden bed (a loan from a newlywed church lady) and a small chest of drawers stood on the concrete floor, softened only by a thin rug in front of the bed.

After four years away, the relocated school felt foreign, and I spent most of my time that summer with my family. Gloria and Ed and their two children were living in the old school building. My parents and the old people were in the gray cottage that had once been the girls' dorm. Walking between the two buildings one day, my mother stopped me beside a peace rose she had planted beside the old dinner bell. We gazed at the perfect light-pink blossom, its velvet petals edged in gold.

"I love it. It's so beautiful," I gushed.

At Mount Moriah, my parents intended forever home, my mother had nurtured a whole garden of tea roses. Now, one rose in an overgrown patch sufficed. My parents were too old and poor to rebuild their lives. Was it too late for me, too, now facing only a small dorm room? And Gloria and Ed were living in the old school building after Leon summoned them from Milwaukee. Were we all fated to never have our own homes or enough money for more than a poor man's rations?

I needed a part-time job before I began teaching high school. I was used to having no money, but I had a car now. During my senior year of college, I'd spotted an ad in the *Chicago Tribune*: a 1957 Volkswagen Bug for $300, the exact amount I had in savings from my hospital aide job. That Saturday night Leon drove me to a dimly lit street where a group of men clustered around the parked VW.

"Maybe we should leave," I whispered, clutching my purse.

Leon got out; I locked the doors. This was not how I'd imagined buying my first car. He knocked on my window. "We'll test-drive it. See how it sounds."

I had no idea how a car should sound, but I nervously got out of the car and walked over to the VW. I slid into the passenger seat, staring at the gear stick rising from the floor. "I can't drive that!" I burst out.

I drove Leon's car back to my rented room in Chicago while he parked my new-to-me Volkswagen Bug at the curb.

Winter revealed a broken gas gauge and a dead heater in my little car. When a snow plow buried it under an icy mountain, I begged Leon to take it away. He drove it to Potomac and in the spring traded it for a sleek, white 1961 Chevy Impala with a silver stag emblem on the hood. Pride swelled in me as I drove to Danville, Illinois, and landed a weekend job at St. Elizabeth's Hospital's psychiatric ward. The drive back and forth from Danville to Potomac wasn't too bad.

Throughout the fall months, I balanced my love for teaching with growing apprehension about the internal workings of the school. Everything was dependent on the will of one man, Leon Graham. Every decision, no matter how small, had to be run past him. Every dollar I needed for chemicals or supplies for chemistry class had to come from him. During college, I had numbed myself to weekend dysphoria, but now I was facing him at every turn. I couldn't revert to seeing him as my trusted counselor or God's truth-bearer. My only relief was knowing my science lab was at the opposite end of the building from his office, and if I were lucky, I could go whole days without having to talk to him.

Thanksgiving dinner at the old folks' home felt sparse. Only four elderly residents remained—three men and a bedridden woman my mother cared for in the room off the kitchen where the old refrigeration unit had stood. The bright paint that welcomed me in 1953 had faded to a dull gray. No funds existed for upkeep. My heart ached for them all. And who would care for my penniless, homeless parents in their frailty?

That Friday, we ate birthday cake in Gloria's kitchen. My mother turned 65, and I was leaving my twenties behind. "Our birthdays are special this year," my mother said innocently.

I forced a smile as the pain of entering my thirties with no prospect of finding a husband tightened the screws. Gloria's chocolate cake stuck in my throat until my eight-year-old niece, Gracie, tugged my arm: "When are you coming to tell our story?"

She and her brother, Gary, were the closest I'd ever come to having children of my own. We cuddled on the parlor couch, the room with the cement slab that read, "The Truth Will Make You Free." I spun a continuing tale to them of underground adventure for "MaPa," a three-eyed witch who was mother, father, and grandparent all in one.

Back in my room that evening, my eyes fell on the square white gift box I'd left on my bed. Leon had stopped me before Thanksgiving break and handed it to me. "Birthday gift," he'd said. "Annie picked it out. I hope you like it."

Alone, I unwrapped the tissue paper to reveal a round orange vase. What was I meant to do with this? Display it? Drown it? I kicked it under my bed.

The next week, I confronted him. I went to his office, the orange vase still fresh on my mind, a bitter symbol of my empty life.

"You have to fix this," I demanded, my voice tight. "I'm angry. I'm tired of living a lie."

He tried to leave, but I blocked him. Then he slipped past me and walked out, leaving me standing in the gloom. I ran after him and planted myself in front of the hood of his truck. I moved away when I saw a student. And Leon drove away.

I had repeated my request to fix this time after time, but what was the use? I was mired in shame. If the truth will make you free, I could never be free.

Was I willing to live a lie so the church women would keep giving him money? Was I keeping silent to protect his reputation, to keep his family from falling apart? I had let him follow me to college, not to protect me but to protect himself. Just when I might have found my freedom, I let him pull me into his world of endless deception, secrecy, and submission. But somewhere, somehow the power was shifting. I didn't need him nearly as much as he needed me to keep quiet.

I passed the student as I hurried to my car and left for my weekend job at the hospital. Like all church workers, I earned no salary at the school. I taught for stars in my crown, except there was no crown—only weary souls reaching for what comfort they could find, believing what they'd been told and trying to survive a hard, uncertain world. Stars might help. I liked stars. I liked constellations, planets, and space. Placing myself as one small dot in the universe, a whisper in eternity, might help me make sense of my life.

By the time I clocked in at the hospital, I felt steadier. My nursing training from my first two years of college had made it easy to get hired as an aide. Friday and Saturday nights were always short-staffed. I entered the dim lobby. The gift shop was closed. The woman at the front desk didn't look up. I rang the bell.

Nick opened the heavy double doors with a grin. "What's up?"

"Same old," I said, stepping through.

The lights were already dimmed on the ward. Patients waited for the medicine that would ease them into sleep in a place where they would be safe for the night.

Nick walked to the ping-pong table. I grabbed my paddle. I liked Nick. He told commune stories surprisingly familiar to mine—shared meals, shared lives, the good and bad together. The difference was how we found our "highs." His came from drugs; mine came from God.

Nick wore bell-bottoms. His brown hair was long and shaggy. I still had on the green dress I'd taught in that day. I'd never worn jeans or pants in my life. In college, I'd stopped braiding and pinning my hair up, defying a church rule. My long hair, once a mark of my faith, was finally in style.

Nick's stories made me laugh. There was the yoga girl with the long blonde hair who was always in trouble. And then there was the music—"Stairway to Heaven," "Rocket Man." I didn't know the songs, but it made me smile when I thought about that stairway to heaven.

My ball shot past him just as the ward doors opened. Only emergencies were admitted on weekends.

We left our ping-pong game as a young woman was wheeled in, her face turned into the pillow, legs drawn up in a fetal position. She was lucky someone had found her and cared enough to bring her in. The doctor waited at the nurse's station. She'd be okay. She would have another day, another chance.

I paused. Lucky? Did I just think that? Yes. But also no. She was safe, but the fight ahead would be hers alone. Piece by piece, she'd have to rebuild herself. I stopped like I'd seen a light on the road to Damascus.

In her, I saw myself. No one could fix me. Not Leon. Not my parents. Not even God, unless I acted first. I had to own my life; I had to dig out, one bit at a time.

Back at the ping-pong table, Nick and I played again. The ball bounced, bumped, and flew. Nick won, but I'd have my turn tomorrow.

Nights on the psych ward were usually just about winning a ping-pong game, but nights like this one reminded me that no one escapes the truth. We are all cracked open by something. Could escaping through that crack set me free?

After my last shift, I drove out into the cold night alone on the road. I savored the sharp air, the bare trees, the distant lights. My heart was lifting.

I was in a safe place. I had a job I loved. I was broken, but I could fix myself.

A thought drifted through me, just out of reach. It was something about the standoff in front of Leon's truck. We were locked in a power struggle. But something was shifting. I would step out of his game to claim the win, even if I didn't yet know how.

This was my life now—my story. I couldn't rebuild myself while clinging to what broke me. Fixing myself didn't mean blaming myself. It meant owning my journey. I would dig myself out of this mess, one bit at a time.

By spring, it was clear Leon wouldn't help me fix anything. My rage was useless, but I was beginning to look outside my small world. "Let's go somewhere for spring break," I begged my parents. "I'll drive."

My mother suggested visiting my father's sister, Aunt Muriel, my sister's namesake. After high school, she had canvassed and taught at the Bible School for the Metropolitan Church. At forty, she was sent back to Connecticut to care for her parents, later marrying a minister but too old for the children she craved. Now they pastored a Tennessee hill-country church. Why had it taken my father decades to reconnect with such a kindred soul?

I battled my demons on those winding roads. Aunt Muriel had been fortunate to find a good husband, though she was well past child-bearing age. Unless I changed my life's path, even marriage seemed unlikely. One conviction crystallized: If my "Mr. Right" existed, I'd better start looking.

Chapter 50
Moving On

All I had to do was tell Leon I wanted to talk to him to upset the equilibrium of his day. Now, locked in what felt like a life-and-death struggle, he would change his schedule to accommodate me. What I was not counting on that day was that our meeting would change the course of my life. We both knew the school wasn't big enough for both of us. I had accepted that I would never speak out and destroy his position and the innocence of the students, my family, his family, and the aging church members. I wanted out, but with hope shrinking with each passing milestone, how could I make it on my own? Would my parents cut me off as they had my sisters if I left? And there was the matter of money. Even on the strictest budget with my hospital job, I couldn't just walk away into a new life.

As I entered Leon's office, he began shuffling papers. "Something came in the mail that you might be interested in." He held out an opened envelope. "You might want to look it over."

I glanced at the letterhead: Association of Christian Schools. Back in my room, I unfolded the paper. It was a listing of openings for teachers in Christian schools across the country. I studied it. One listing called my name. Would I really be able to start over, find my way, and meet the man my heart longed for? A school in Virginia was looking for a science and math teacher for grades seven and eight. I was licensed for grades seven through twelve.

My reply expressing interest was in the mail the next morning. Norfolk Christian School flew me out for an interview, and I had a job. With Leon engineering my departure and a Christian school as the destination, no alarm bells were triggered for my parents or Gloria. I was finally on my way out.

At the end of the summer on the Friday before Norfolk Christian School opened its doors for the 1972–73 year, I headed east in my white Chevy Impala, a paper map with its array of red and blue roads unfolded on the seat beside me. This time I had a job lined up, an apartment, a roommate, and a new church. I was poised for success. I would fit into a Christian school with my modest dresses and appearance. No one would know of my struggles, my strange church, or my shame.

I knew the salary was about half of what public school teachers made, but $4,500 was a staggering amount to me. As I drove, I remembered my student teaching in Chicago. I'd been assigned to an affluent suburb in North Chicago where the teachers wore designer fashions and expensive shoes, and students seemed to show up in new outfits every day. My attempts to socialize in the teachers' lounge had left me cringing. My mentor teacher was appalled that my goal was to teach, unpaid, in a small, nondescript Christian school, but I tried to explain that I would rather teach with little monetary reward than at a school where I'd be forever an outsider.

I crossed into the state of Virginia around 5:00 in the afternoon with more miles still to go. Was it because I was tired that my mind fell into the dark place I had been resisting all day? Why did I do it?

The question nagged me. Why did I give Leon my phone number and address when he asked for it? Nothing good could come of it.

"I will call you," he said. "I will call every Sunday so you don't have to call me."

So I wouldn't call him, of course. I still had the power to dump a can of worms into his lap by calling at an inappropriate time.

"Pick a name we will use," he directed.

I agreed that "Ken" would call me every Sunday evening at five o'clock.

He knew my weakness. He knew that whenever I needed guidance, I relied on him. Even now, I wasn't sure I was ready to face the future alone. How could I know I wouldn't run into a problem in Virginia that would stop me in my tracks?

The next morning, sunlight picked out the bright pink roses on the upholstery covers in the living room of my new apartment. My roommate, Judy, had graduated from Bob Jones University and was looking forward to her first job teaching sixth grade. I hoped I came across as a confident, seasoned teacher, even if it was only a mirage.

Smiles greeted us as we entered Norfolk Christian Church on Sunday morning, and the congregation clapped as new and returning teachers were introduced. I glanced around and took a deep breath. I was ready to welcome new scenery on the road to heaven. My sisters and brother had embraced this denomination, and I would make it mine. I would arrive at the pearly gates if I adhered to what I was hearing from this pulpit just as surely as if I remained in my own church.

After the service, the pastor invited Judy and me to dinner at the parsonage. Two little girls with long dark curls down their backs and puffy dresses danced into the parlor, offering us glasses of sweet tea. I was hearing "yes ma'am" for the first time. Two little boys with big brown eyes peeked around the corner, staring at us as their father and an older boy entered the room.

"I want you to meet Timothy," the preacher said. "He'll be one of your eighth-grade students. Timothy collects memorabilia from the Civil War and wants to show you his treasures while we wait for dinner."

Timothy led us down the hall to his room. I looked at two tarnished swords with brass handles, a rusty canteen with the chain still attached, and an assortment of cannonballs. "We found these cannonballs on our summer vacations in a cabin in the hills," the pastor explained. "The school takes the older students on a field trip every spring to the battlefield at Richmond." I looked at the small Confederate flag displayed with the collection and was left wondering which side had won that battle. I was quickly picking up that south of the Mason-Dixon Line, the Civil War still lingered.

"What are you young ladies planning for the afternoon?" the Reverend asked as we finished our meal of fried chicken, followed by pecan pie.

"I'm going out to collect dirt," I answered. "I'm teaching soil types in my first lesson tomorrow." I planned to lay out chunks of hard clay like the garden soil in Union Grove, and I hoped to find rich loam from the banks along the river.

"How about I take you out to look for dirt?" the pastor offered. "I might know some places."

And that's how I ended up riding in the passenger seat in the minister's car that afternoon. "We'll stop near the river first," he said.

At the riverbank, I scooped light brown sand into my cardboard shoebox. Next, we stopped at the edge of a stand of yellow pine. That dirt, too, was sandy, breaking apart in damp clumps. We drove to several other spots, hoping for better samples, but it was all the same: wet and grainy sand. I was the one learning about soil near the ocean, and my students would only hear me describe the rich black loam and sticky gray clay I remembered from the Midwest.

On the way back to the church, the pastor broke the silence. "Have you thought about getting married?"

The question blindsided me. Alarm surged through me—shock, confusion, a pang of anger. I wanted to disappear. "No," I said too quickly. What else could I say? My longing was buried too deep to offer up to a stranger, especially a preacher.

"Don't you want children someday?" he asked, "like my little boys, David and Jonathan?"

I looked out the window, fighting back tears. This man had no idea what kind of life I had come from or what had driven me to this unfamiliar town, this unfamiliar church, this awkward car ride. He had no right to reach into the deepest part of me and poke at dreams I barely allowed myself to admit.

And yet I had lied—flat out lied. I had once told my fifth-grade class in Union Grove that I was a Yankee, and Yankees don't lie. Now here I was, a Yankee in the Old South, committing a quiet betrayal of myself, my heritage, and my soul. But who even asked questions like that?

Only later did it sink in. My answer had slammed the door shut on any hope I'd had of fulfilling my longing for love and family within his church. But how could he possibly

understand me? What was I even doing in a car alone with a married preacher?

I was digging up sand. I realized the answer was prophetic. I was hoping to find something solid, but all I kept pulling up was sand that wouldn't hold its shape.

Chapter 51
Virginia

I carried my box of sand up to the apartment. "Judy," I called, "I have a friend back in Illinois who says he's going to call me at five o'clock tonight. Ken is his name."

She was looking through her stack of books for the sixth grade. "No problem," she answered.

The phone rang at exactly five o'clock. The cord was long enough to pull it into my room. "Yes, I had a good trip. Yes, I like my roommate." I sat on the floor, my back against the door, still reeling from the questioning that afternoon. I could never repeat it. It was sealed forever in the saddest corner of my heart.

I stayed on the floor holding the phone after he hung up. I needed to hear his voice, to know he was thinking of me, even if he wished he could free himself of me. He was a lifeline I desperately grasped. Would I ever be brave enough to face the unknown without a safety line? I would block out the dark parts of our relationship, and he would remain the friend I needed. With a thousand miles between us, how could it go wrong?

"I am having a great time teaching out here," I told him as the weeks passed. "I really found my niche with the seventh and eighth graders. I've started working on my master's degree at Old Dominion. I'm enjoying my classes."

One Sunday night, I told him I was going to North Carolina to visit my Aunt Muriel and Uncle Charles. They had moved from Tennessee to a town south of Asheville and were only three hours away. "I saw on the map that I will drive through Durham and Chapel Hill," I said. "You could fly out to see me." I threw the idea out playfully, not dreaming he would take me up on it. How he arranged his schedule, found the money, and arrived at the destination just as I was driving there remains a mystery.

I showed off my little green and white Ford Maverick. One Sunday night I had told him about the loud knocking in the engine of my Impala. I was proud of myself for navigating the trade, especially since I learned about credit ratings for the first time and realized I had none.

We were getting ready to leave when he told me he had to call, Helen, the canvassing manager in Chicago, to tell her he'd be arriving late in Chicago. I sat on the bed waiting for him. He was still carrying on the Saturday night visits to Race Street and still preaching at the little building in the alley on Sunday mornings.

"Dorie," I heard him speak my name into the phone.

I jumped, my eyes wide.

"I mean Helen," he quickly corrected himself. That slip sent warning shivers jolting through me. He had become careless. The unraveling was set in motion.

For another year I tried to find myself in Virginia. But I had no friends, certainly no boyfriend, and I was awash with questions about my soul.

One spring day, I walked the few blocks to a point of land on the Lafayette River and sat on a bench, watching the seagulls and gazing into the choppy water. This was not where I belonged. I was an outsider looking in, seeking but not finding people like my people. I missed the selfless saints like my mother. I wanted the voice of authority, even when I knew it was false. I was still hanging on to the baggage of my past, and the buried dream of my future was just as far out of reach as when I began my quest.

I was not going to join the church in Norfolk, and I was not going to find my man in Virginia. I would go back—not to the church, not to Leon, but to my family.

"I'll meet you at the state line before crossing into Illinois," Leon told me in our last five o'clock phone call before I left Virginia. I agreed. Why did he want to meet me? Was he worried I was encroaching on his space again? Was he finally calling an end to this convoluted saga?

If he had something to tell me, I did not discover it when we met at the Illinois border. We did not discuss the future or the past. We met, two souls in a worn-out relationship, clinging helplessly to tattered threads. Neither one wanted it, but the end continued to elude us.

Chapter 52
Indianapolis

The year after Virginia, I taught at a large Christian high school in Indianapolis, Indiana. That year, I turned thirty-three. I did not talk to Leon at all that year. I didn't miss it. I didn't need it. I didn't want it. But angst, isolation, and dissonance lingered. I did not find a place in the church in Indianapolis, quickly discovering that with over a thousand members, no one was keeping track of whether I attended or not.

Every Friday after school, I drove the 100 miles to Potomac where my parents had moved into a two-bedroom cottage after the old people were gone. The house needed a new roof and a new furnace, and the windows rattled and leaked cold air in the winter. There was no money from the church to repair it. My mother trusted the Lord to provide, but my father struggled. He wrote a letter to Leon, asking for the right to remain in the cottage permanently.

My father had taken a handyman job at a nearby nursing home to pay the bills, but there was little money left for repairs to the cottage. I brought bags of groceries when I came home.

My father wasn't the only one struggling. My mother told me of the times Gloria came over, rested her head on the table, and wept over the condition of the church. Wherever she went, she had started a Sunday school, but now there was no Sunday school for her children at Potomac. The only preaching service was Sunday evening, and it was directed to the young people at the school. "Leon has forgotten us," she told my mother.

One Saturday, I locked my room in Indianapolis, a small attic room like the one I'd had in college. School was out for the summer, and I was headed for the familiar Illinois countryside I loved. I drove through woods lining the road in shades from lime to hunter green, past plowed fields where corn or soybeans were pushing up, covering the ground with a soft green mantle. I crossed the Wabash River, its banks swollen with spring runoff whooshing its way under the bridge.

I had finished my master's degree the previous summer, and this summer I was going home because I had nothing else to do and no money to do it with. When I entered the house with my little blue suitcase, my mother met me with an exuberant hug, fretting as usual about the bed in my room. "I'm so sorry about that old mattress," she said, "but they don't make them that size anymore. I wish the sheets fit better."

"Don't worry," I told her. "I'm just thankful for a place to stay." I unpacked in my little shoebox of a room, hanging my clothes on a rack against the wall opposite the bed. The iron bedstead was three-quarter size, between a double and a twin, and had been part of our furniture since Union Grove. At one end of the dark little room was the door to the kitchen. At the other end was a sturdy door that led to the glassed-in back porch. At some point, the room had been shrunken to add a bathroom to the house. The only external light came from a window in the door to the porch. When I pulled the chain on the lamp, faded little yellow roses appeared on the dark red wallpaper.

My mother was fixing lunch when I stepped into the kitchen a few minutes later. Starched white curtains framed the window, and the walls were yellow. "That's the color a kitchen should be," my mother always said. She had painted the kitchen yellow wherever she settled.

"Look what we have," she beamed, motioning toward the sink. It was full of pink radishes and bright green lettuce leaves. "You're here to celebrate the first vegetables from the garden." It took so little to make her happy. I saw my father coming up the front steps. He was seventy-two, dressed as always in his blue and white striped overalls with his faded cap perched on his full head of grey hair.

"I see you've been busy in the garden," I greeted him, setting the radishes on the table. My father was happiest when he was pushing his big wheel cultivator between the rows. He chuckled.

"I have my eye on the spinach; it'll be next."

We sat down at the table and bowed our heads. "Please bless this food, and thank you that Dorie is home," my father prayed.

The word *home* hit me with painful irony. I loved my parents, but I was here because I had nowhere else to go. I should have had my own home by now, but I was still coming back to my parents.

"Leon came over to see Ed while I was in the garden last night," my father said as he heaped lettuce on his plate. "I heard them talking money, as usual." The agitation in his voice was jarring. "You can't squeeze blood from a turnip. It's about time he did something besides talk."

"Please pass the radishes," my mother jumped in to change the subject. My father reached for the vinegar cruet.

"You still eat vinegar and sugar on your lettuce?" I smiled. "I remember when you fixed mine like that and cut it up for me."

"Been eating it like that all my life," my father said.

"Don't mind your father," my mother said as we washed dishes after the meal. "He has a lot on his mind. He doesn't want to put money into a new roof on this house if the church is just going to move us again. Leon hasn't answered that letter to give us permission to stay here as long as we need to," she sighed. "It's so sad. Leon seems unaware that we exist. I'm so happy we have our little church in Danville."

In an almost inconceivable shift, my sister Gloria had begun taking her children to an "outside" church in Danville for Sunday school. Like sand filling a void, my parents soon began attending with her, and even Ed was going on Sunday mornings. I had evaded church completely that year.

"Oh," my mother added, "we've been having revival meetings at the church all week. The preacher is an old holiness man, eighty-four years old, but my, can he preach. Tonight is family night, and I hope you'll go with us."

That night, my mother's voice rang out rich and full as we sang the old-time hymns. The Lord's Prayer was recited in the words I was familiar with, having memorized them back in the Bible School. The service was, as she said, a celebration of the Christian family. Did my parents remember that I had never heard a sermon like that growing up? I had believed fractured families were normal, that children were destined to rebel and be forced out if they did not work for the church. Now I was listening to a preacher pleading with young people to seek God's guidance in choosing a life partner. He was saying that choosing a life partner was part of God's plan, that love didn't have to come cloaked in secrecy or shame. I sat frozen in my seat, my hands clenched in my lap. What if I had been given that kind of hope?

I glanced over at Gloria's children, their small heads drooping with sleep. They were safe. They would grow up in a better world than I had. And for that, I was grateful.

The next morning, my suitcase lay open on a chair, and I averted my eyes from the object crammed into its corner. Finally, I reached for it and shook out the sweater I had knit years before, its yoke a Nordic pattern with white snowflakes on a red and green background, the body dark ivory. I should have thrown it away long ago, but I didn't. When I started knitting it, I knew Leon couldn't wear it. That was why I never gave it to him when it was finished.

As I pulled it out, all the memories came flooding back—painful memories of the time I thought I loved him and thought he loved me. Then it hit me. My transformation was complete. I was not that person anymore. But I still wanted him to see what I had worked on for countless hours while thinking of him. He had to see the intricate pattern I was proud of and see that none of it mattered anymore.

It had taken ten years, but finally I had a course of action. I would call him to come over.

I was waiting on the back porch with the sweater in my hand when he pulled up at exactly eight o'clock the next morning. Rays of bright morning sunshine streamed through the windows, making the dust particles sparkle. The only furniture was a freezer chest and a white metal table where my father started tomato and pepper seeds. It was cleaned off now, the wooden boxes empty and neatly stacked.

"Here's the sweater I knit for you," I said, holding it out as he entered the room and closed the door behind him. He shrank back as if I were holding a weapon.

"I can't take that," he said, desperation spilling into his voice.

"But I made it for you," I taunted. "I spent hours and hours knitting it for you." He winced. I saw his confusion. "I made it for you," I repeated, more forcefully, stepping closer to him with the sweater. At fifty-two, he seemed to have aged significantly in the last year. The aura of power was gone from his stance. His eyes lacked warmth, and the frown lines had deepened on his face.

"I don't want it," he said, backing away. I threw the sweater in his face. He put up his hands, and it fell to the floor. I stepped forward, picked it up, and threw it at him again.

"Take it and get rid of it. I don't want it. It's yours. Throw it in the trash."

He caught it. I began to close the distance between us, making him back up toward the door. "It's trash," I repeated. "Throw it away."

He turned and walked to his truck. I watched him drive away with the sweater. I was shaking, and anger coursed through me. As my breathing slowed, the new reality began to sink in. It was over. There would be no more meetings. I opened the door to my dark little room and closed the suitcase.

I went to work with my father that summer, filling in for vacationing staff at the nursing home. His car was running on a prayer, already old when it was allotted to him by the church ten years ago. I listened as he worried about the car, about the house, and even about the nursing home's financial troubles. He feared that he would lose his job.

I began looking at cars in the evening paper. Then I went to a Volkswagen showroom and chose a little bright yellow Bug that matched the dandelions in the grass. It was my happy color, evoking warm sunshine and smiley faces. I gave the Ford Maverick to my father. The weight of his burdens eased a bit. I also bought a small television. My parents had been married fifty years, and this was their first contact with the airwaves. We sat together in the evenings cheering on Ernie Banks and the Chicago Cubs baseball team.

Chapter 53
Taking Control

Before I headed back to Indianapolis for another year of teaching, I stopped at my sister's to take my niece and nephew shopping for school.

"Be good for Auntie," Gloria called as we pulled out. We shopped, stopped for ice cream, and shopped some more.

"Take your bags into the other room," Gloria said, sounding tired as she shooed her children out of the kitchen when we returned. She turned away from me toward the sink.

"Is something wrong?" I waited for her to speak. I seldom saw her feelings so much on display.

"It's Ed," she was crying. "Tomorrow the church convention starts, and he says he's going over every day because Leon needs him. I just want him to be through with that church, but there's nothing I can do."

"You can keep doing what you're doing and take Mom and Dad and the kids to church in Danville." It was all I could offer.

Gloria wiped her eyes. "Leon came over again this afternoon. It's all Leon, Leon, Leon. I understand the church members are looking for a good convention, but I hoped Ed would tell Leon no this time."

I didn't want to leave Gloria, but she told me to go home. "There's nothing we can do," she said.

Clouds were thickening for a storm as I got into my car. The key was poised over the ignition, but I didn't start the engine. I sat like that, holding my breath. Then I jumped out of the car and ran back up the steps into the kitchen. "I need to talk to Ed." I raced through the room to the basement door before my sister could stop me.

Fifteen years ago when I was a student in this building, Ed had been one of my favorite teachers. What would he think now if I told him the truth?

Cool air struck my face as I opened the basement door and ran down the stairs. The printing press stood in the middle of one of the basement rooms. The room had not been restored; gray plaster cracked and peeled on the walls. On one side was a large fireplace, still with marble panels. The windows on two sides were dark with the approaching storm. In front of the nonfunctioning fireplace, Ed sat at his desk with a paper in his hand. The wrinkles in his forehead between his eyes touched, and I could see the tired slump of his shoulders.

Seeing him brought a sick feeling and the urge to run back up the stairs. "I have to talk to you," I said, trying to control the tremor in my voice.

Ed looked at me. Something in my tone alerted him. He laid down the paper and waited. A long silence followed as I struggled to speak. Finally, I continued. "I have to tell you about Leon and me. Leon isn't who you think he is," my confession tumbled out. My words would crush Ed, and my reputation would be in tatters. "You can't trust him," I continued. "He came up to Chicago early every Saturday when I was in college just to see me. He came out when I was in Virginia too."

My confession followed and then there was silence. Ed's voice was breaking when he finally spoke. "What are you saying?" His question landed heavily between us. "When did this start?"

"After Linda died, but just before I went to college, there was a kiss."

Ed was the most loyal person I had ever met. His loyalty to Leon and commitment to the church were the cornerstones of his life. "I'll talk to Leon," he finally said, and added, "Thank you for what you just told me." I heard genuine empathy in his voice.

He startled me by standing up, and I backed away. "We'll talk tomorrow," he said.

"Okay," I said, turning and almost running out of the room.

What had I just done? I had exposed the wreck of my life and left it lying open in plain sight. My image was shattered, and there would be consequences. If Ed didn't follow through with probing into what I had told him, what would I do? Tears spilled from my eyes as the cycle of hopelessness and shame gripped me. Would Ed be angry that I had not told him sooner, or that I told him at all?

As I stepped outside, the sky opened up, and I slid quickly into my car. Thunder crashed, and the rain fell in torrents. The summer storm would give respite from the heat, and tomorrow would dawn bright and fresh. Was it possible the same could be my story? The windshield wipers beat in time with my aching heart.

Chapter 54
Board Meeting

The next day, I pulled into the parking lot of the church school where the annual church convention was held, steering around puddles from last night's rain. The air was already steamy as the August sun bore down on me at eight o'clock in the morning. The grounds were park-like, and clusters of old friends stood in the shade of the trees, catching up after a year of canvassing for the church.

Ed waited for me at the door of the school building. I took a deep breath, mentally repeating my mantra: You can do this. Early that morning, Ed had called and asked me to present my story to the board, just as I had told him. I had never envisioned such a platform for my confession, and though I thought of refusing, I realized that if I were ever to move on from my past and embrace my future, now was the moment. This was my chance for redemption. Things could go wrong, but it was a risk I had to take. Ed believed me, but would the board? How would they react when I revealed the deception and lies of the past decade?

"Leon has not shown his face. Just tell them what you told me last night." There was a heavy sadness in Ed's voice.

The board members were seated in a circle. They were all familiar to me, but I could not read their expressions as they looked up. Two men sat beside an old preacher with white curly hair and bushy white eyebrows. One of the men held a stenographer's tablet; this meeting would be recorded. There was an empty chair between Ed and Helen. She was not on the board, but I understood why she'd been invited. She would corroborate my confession about those Saturday nights at Race Street when I was in college. Ed motioned to the empty chair. He was the vice president of the church and formally opened the meeting.

"As you all know, I talked to Leon last night after Dorie came to me. I told him that unless he could explain what had occurred and tell us his side, he should not show up. Since he hasn't come, I assume he will not be present for the remainder of the convention."

I was holding my breath, sweat already beading on my forehead as Ed turned to me.

"Dorie, I'm asking you to repeat what you told me last night."

I looked down at my clenched fists, not wanting to register looks of disbelief or abhorrence that might appear on the faces around me.

As I hesitated, the white-haired preacher spoke up. "When did this begin?"

My mind went back to Linda's death and the wreck I was. "He supported me then," I began, "and it just kept getting more involved. He left notes with the first letter of each word for 'I shall always love you.' I told myself it was *pure* love, but when he wanted my little red silk scarf, the one I tied around my neck so he could smell it when he was traveling, it didn't feel right. I gave it to him anyway. Then, the summer before I went to college, he took me to the beach in Brownsville, Texas, one night and kissed me. He said, 'I just can't let you go.'"

My eyes begged Ed to let me stop, silently pleading for a break. The room was filled with silence, and the men leaned in. Ed asked me to go on.

"And at girls' camp . . ." I recounted the molestation, uncertain if they'd believe me. "I struggled to see him as my mentor and spiritual advisor. I couldn't tell anyone. All the people of the church believed in him, and my parents were part o

I took a few deep breaths and then continued. "Then college started, and it was such a new experience. He came for me every Saturday, and I thought I needed him. I would follow him to Race Street. He came down to the basement where I slept." I glanced at Helen sitting beside me. "I'm so sorry." Tears spilled from my eyes. She was the face of all the women of the church I had betrayed. I couldn't go on. Helen slipped me her handkerchief, and I struggled to catch my breath.

"Helen, do you remember a couple years ago when he phoned you to tell you he would be late, and he called you Dorie?"

"Yes, I do," she answered without hesitation, her tone unmistakably clear. "I wondered about that."

"He had come out to see me when I was in Virginia. We were at a motel near the airport." I frantically pressed the handkerchief to my eyes.

After a long silence, the white-haired man spoke. "Thank you for your bravery in sharing your story with us," he said. "We don't blame you for this. I'm deeply sorry it happened to you."

I stood, and Ed walked with me outside. Unable to speak, I got into my car as he thanked me again. Despite my tears, I wanted to drive away. But as I gripped the steering wheel, my emotions shifted. Anger, a fierce rage, dried my tears. Leon should have been the one admitting the enormity of it and taking the blame. I felt guilty, but not to the extent he should have. I drove back to town, burning with anger and resentment.

When my parents returned from church in Danville, I was careful to steer the conversation toward the coming school year as we ate lunch. I hoped they hadn't heard, but I knew Gloria would tell them. How could she help it? I kept my eyes on my plate, making sure to smile when appropriate. I couldn't risk a single word slipping out.

They didn't ask, not yet. But I saw the way my mother's brow furrowed when she thought I wasn't looking. My father, unusually quiet, buttered his roll in slow, methodical strokes. Maybe they already knew. Maybe they didn't want to know.

One thing was certain: I would never discuss today's business with them. Not ever.

Chapter 55
Walking Out

I drove back to Indianapolis to my little upstairs rented room near Garfield Park. Tomorrow was orientation at Indianapolis Christian High School and I sorted out my school supplies and picked the outfit I would wear. My mother had made it for me, a two-piece skirt and top with a black background and scattered multicolored flowers. Like all teachers, I was excited for a new school year but sad that summer was ending. Still, something was eating at me. Was a new free spirit awakening in me? Was I still a fit for a Christian school, or was a long-suppressed urge to walk free from religious restraints beginning to stir?

"Doris!" The principal called my name as I walked in the door that Monday morning. "Come into my office for a minute."

Standing in front of his desk, I heard him say, "You will be teaching chemistry this year."

Of course, I could teach chemistry, but I knew the moment he said those words that they had not hired a science teacher to take Mrs. Markowski's place. She had taught chemistry and physics last year, but she had moved away. That meant I would be teaching all the high school science classes.

"I can't do that," I burst out. There was no way I would allow myself to become the entire science department. This was not a small school, and my classes last year had been large. Labs, especially chemistry labs, took extra preparation time. While I dithered, he answered me.

"You can and you will."

I stumbled out of his office. "You can and you will" echoed in my head as I worked that morning. I knew science teachers were in short supply, and the school had simply been unable to find a replacement. But that didn't make his ultimatum any more palatable. In his words, I heard the voice of the church that had controlled me all my life. The principal was not delivering a church decree, but he had taken away my voice. Had I just freed myself from the bondage of my church only to submit to another controlling force? How could he be so dismissive of my feelings?

I walked out of the high school as the orientation session ended for lunch. On my way out, I looked up the address for the Indianapolis Public School Headquarters. "You can and you will" was etched in my mind, but a new mantra began to take shape. "I am free," I whispered to myself. "I am free," I repeated as I walked up the steps to the administration building. The limestone blocks sparkled a dazzling white in the noon sunshine. As I stepped inside, my eyes adjusted to the darkness inside the foyer. It was empty. With my heart thumping, I walked down the hall toward an open door. An African American man looked up from where he was sitting at a massive desk.

"I am a biology teacher," I declared. "I need a job."

"We are short two biology teachers. Come in and tell me about yourself." His tone was welcoming, in contrast to the harsh manner in which I had been told just a few hours earlier that I would be doubling my teaching load.

"If you can break your contract, you have a job," he said. I had not signed a contract, and the vision of being free from religious constraints propelled me back to my car and back to the school.

"I will not be teaching for you this year," I told the principal in my most assertive tone. "Adding chemistry to my already full load is not feasible."

Chapter 56
Tasting Freedom

I don't remember the rest of the conversation with the principal, if there was more. I recall returning to the public schools' administration building for the second time. There I signed a contract for a biology position in an Indianapolis public high school.

Nothing could shake my sense of empowerment as I began my new job. My salary had doubled from $6,000 to $12,000, more money than I had ever seen in my life. More importantly, no one was looking over my shoulder to uncover the falsehoods that had defined me. I was teaching biology at Broad Ripple High School, only five periods a day.

What will happen to my parents? Intrusive thoughts about their plight crowded in when I was not busy with school. I was responsible if they lost their house. It was because I told. I was still going home on weekends as I had the year before, and I had begun attending their new church in Danville during the summer. What had initially felt like euphoric freedom from religious oppression just weeks ago was turning into a bewildering rabbit hole. For the first time in my life, no one was in charge of my spiritual journey.

I found myself contemplating my next steps. I still felt I needed a preacher, although I kicked myself for the thought. I needed to find a pastor of our new denomination at a church in Indianapolis and ask for counseling. I drove to a church on the west side and pulled into the parking lot. I sat for a moment studying the small white building with the cross above its wide doors.

I shouldn't be doing this. Warning bells went off in my head, but I walked into the pastor's office. He was an older man nearing retirement age. Surely he would understand. I took a seat across from him. My mind would not stop cycling through my misgivings. Why am I doing this again? Why do I always need someone to spiritually hold my hand and tell me what to do? Memories of praying with Glady with a strange pastor in Connecticut resurfaced. But my heart screamed that I needed someone with a better connection to God to tell me what His will was for me. If God's plan for my life can be resurrected, it will take a holy road map.

The pastor sat back as I began, his hands folded, fingers steepled in front of him. He listened in silence as I told my story, leaving out the parts I could not bring myself to repeat again. I told him about the liaison and about confessing to Ed. I expressed my uncertainty and my need for guidance.

When I finished, I waited. Finally he spoke: "I find it hard to believe you could not leave that situation sooner."

His words stung, and everything else he said faded into the night. I felt judged. How could I explain the years spent in a church where I was financially trapped? And what about the emotional dependency that had been cultivated in me? What about the power dynamics that made it unthinkable for me to speak out? And there was the guilt and shame that kept me bound to dependency. From my story, this is what he had gleaned: I should have been able to escape, and I had failed. I had come seeking guidance, hoping for reassurance that I was now pointed in the right direction. Instead, I was being measured and found lacking.

I rose, not waiting for further discussion or a closing prayer, and walked out. We both knew there were no easy answers to my problems. I did not get approval or guidance. But I had just set myself free from another chain, and with a surge of confidence, I knew I could work things out for myself. No pastor ever again would hear my pitiful story. I was on my own, and I could do it.

After school on Friday, I stopped to buy groceries to take to my parents. I walked, as usual, past the storefronts of the strip mall to the grocery store at the end of the block. Photos of houses and detailed descriptions of real estate in a crowded display window caught my attention. I had passed it so many times without a thought, but this time I stopped and studied the pictures. "Come In," the sign in the window read. "Let us help you find your new home."

I walked in. The woman inside stood, and suddenly I was listening to a sales pitch. "We have a plan for first-time home buyers," she said, questioning me about finances.

"Wait," I interrupted her. "I am on my way to the grocery store. Let me think about it and come back later."

As I made the two-hour drive to Potomac, my mind was racing with the thought of buying a house for my parents.

Chapter 57
Equal Opportunity Act

When I arrived at Potomac, my mother was warming up a kettle of salmon chowder, leftovers from supper the night before. When I sat down at the kitchen table, I was on pins and needles to tell her about my visit to the real estate office and my plan to buy a house. But that would have to wait until we joined my father in the living room. The familiar aroma of salmon chowder carried me back to childhood. My mother stood at the stove, stirring the kettle as she had done countless times when I was growing up. Salmon chowder wasn't just food; it was the story of her own childhood, only then it was clam chowder.

Her family would gather at the mouth of the Thames River in Connecticut for picnics. She would join the children who were wading in the mud to dig up quahogs. My grandfather would shuck them, and my grandmother would prepare a big kettle of clam chowder on a fire on the shore. Since we had moved to the Midwest when I was very young, my mother had adapted the chowder to canned salmon. It carried the same love for family and sense of comfort as the clam chowder on the beach.

"Ed has been offered a church," my mother said, sitting down beside me at the table. "It's about 100 miles south of here. They need a pastor, and Ed wants a clean break from the old church."

"Old church" conjured up memories I wanted to forget. I navigated the conversation carefully. I had no intention of discussing my past with my parents, but Gloria had told them about my confession. I tipped my bowl and spooned up the last bit of chowder. As silence filled the room, my mother's voice cut through softly. "I understand why it happened, Dorie. He was a powerful man."

I nearly choked and stood up from the table. We quickly tidied the kitchen and went into the parlor to discuss buying a house with my father. "Well, well," he said, "I didn't know you could do that. You might be biting off more than you can chew."

"I don't know for sure," I answered, "but the Realtor sounded hopeful. I'll find out next week when I take in my financial information." I went to bed with my mind made up that I would find a way to buy a house.

Then my mother's words began to rise in my mind, echoing through my thoughts. She said she understood why it happened. I didn't understand that myself. How could she when I had kept the truth hidden all those years? Was she saying I didn't have to bear the burden alone, that my parents were not judging me? Perhaps this was her way of telling me it was okay to let go of the fear and guilt I had carried for so long.

"He was a powerful man"—I kept turning those five words over in my mind. What did that mean? Tears threatened as I remembered the night I stumbled from his car after the kiss. I was on the threshold of college, seeking freedom and validation at the age of twenty-five.

Suddenly, it flashed before my eyes as though the room lit up. It had never been about romance. It was never about love. From the moment he forced my head onto his lap and under the steering wheel, it had been about power. I thought back to his choice of words: "I can't let you go." What he really meant was "I won't let you go."

But I was not that defenseless young woman anymore. I was ready to move on, confident now that even my family understood. That realization brought release and a sense of peace as I drifted off to sleep.

Driving back to Indianapolis on Sunday afternoon, I considered my mother's words again. She cared. She forgave me. I would buy them a house. But there had to be forgiveness on my part too. As a child who had watched my older sisters be disowned for marrying outside the church and as I had grown up with the odds stacked against me to find my own way, I blamed my parents for not preparing me for adulthood. Staying in the church had exacted a heavy price on all of us. It would take time to heal, but I was on my way.

I returned to the real estate office after school on Monday with all my financial information. I didn't know that two years ago the Equal Opportunity Act had passed, which allowed the Realtor to speak confidently about my getting a loan. Before that, a woman needed her father or a husband to sign for a government loan.

Over the weekend, my parents had shared their home-buying experience, but the only home they had ever bought was in Union Grove. Prices had gone up since my father paid $5,000 with a $1 down payment. I remembered my mother and Eleanor in Union Grove, standing on wood planks balanced between stepladders in the dining room as they pasted wallpaper on the walls. When they finished, my mother stood back, admired their work, and explained to me that by dropping the wallpaper a foot down from the ceiling, it made the 12-foot walls seem not quite so tall. In the winter, my father had tacked plastic sheets on the inside of the windows of that old house to keep in the heat.

After that house, I had only lived in canvassing homes and rented rooms. Some of those houses that I shared with the canvassing ladies after high school were almost as bad. They sagged and creaked; they were too hot in summer and too cold in winter; and the doors wouldn't stay shut. "Please help me find a house in better condition," I prayed.

When the Realtor began to talk about buying a house "as is," I listened carefully. Weren't all houses "as is" when you bought them? All I understood as I sat down at the table was that I had a choice of the houses in a thick, black, loose-leaf binder—all the "as is" houses the government had repossessed.

That night, I called my parents. "I can get a loan for the house," I said, bubbling with excitement.

"We've been thinking about it," my mother replied. I waited; nothing at this point could deter me from home ownership. Finally, it came out. "It's about the church. Daddy and I have been thinking about it," she repeated.

"There are churches here, Mama, of the same denomination," I pointed out. "Try to find a house near a church."

Some things never changed. Of course, I would try for a house near a church in their denomination, but come hell or high water, I was buying a house.

Chapter 58
Ebbie Road

I picked up the business yellow pages and turned to churches. Indianapolis was full of churches, but there were only three in the denomination my parents wanted. I had met the pastor of one, and we weren't moving near that one. I hoped some of the "as is" houses were near the two remaining churches of their denomination.

The Realtor took me out the next evening. We drove through neighborhoods with rows of little houses that looked almost new in my eyes although most had been built in the 1950s. It was nearly dark when we pulled into the driveway of a little red brick ranch-style house, similar to the red brick houses on either side.

"It says the roof and furnace are in good condition in this one," the Realtor said. "Let's take a quick look."

We walked in, and she turned on the lights. The wood paneling in the living room glowed warm and inviting. We looked at the three bedrooms—beautiful in my eyes despite several holes where an angry fist had made contact. The bathroom was nice, and I knew my mother would like the kitchen with room for a table. It was hard to see the backyard since it was dark out, but it was large and enclosed with a fence. My father would be happy.

"This is it," I told the Realtor. I paid $18,000 for my house on Ebbie Road.

I didn't own any dishes or furniture, but my parents would furnish the home. They would be sure to bring my mother's maple bedroom set that had followed them around since they bought it new in Connecticut in 1946. My parents moved in on March 19, 1976, their fifty-first wedding anniversary.

"This is beautiful," my mother said, rubbing her hand across the wood paneling. "The kitchen is so big. This is wonderful."

My father was already out the back door. I joined him. "There's a place for a nice garden in that corner," he pointed. I saw rose bushes around the chain-link fence that made my heart sing.

"Oh," my mother said, inspecting a large hole in the bedroom wall and the splinters around the holes in the cheap doors.

"Nothing we can't fix right away," my father said.

The walls needed paint, the front storm door was broken, and the rug in the living room was worn, but we all agreed it was the best home we had ever had.

My father brought his big-wheel cultivator and all his gardening tools and planting flats. Soon, he was carrying out new little tomato and pepper plants in the morning and bringing them in again in the evening as he hardened them up for the spring planting. I helped my mother paint the bedrooms, and our kitchen glowed bright yellow. White peonies sprang up against the south side of the house as the weather warmed.

My parents found their place in the new church only 2 miles from the house and began attending prayer meetings, fellowships, and Bible studies. I attended with them on Sundays, but there was no singles group. I was too old for the youth group and didn't qualify for the young families group. One Sunday night, I answered the altar call. It was time to tidy up my record in the Judgment Book. My parents were happy.

Chapter 59
Summer Job

That summer, I took a job at a children's home in northern Indiana to help pay my mortgage. I found myself the housemother of six boys—all thirteen and fourteen years old. Two other house parents—single men in their thirties—shared the responsibilities. They moved between houses, but one was always there at night.

"I'll fix you dinner tonight," Charlie said on a night we had off. It was the first time I had eaten fried potatoes with the skins on.

"I'll take you to the state park tomorrow to hike," Michael said on his night at the house.

Charlie gave me a small blue book, *The Little Prince*, his favorite as a child.

Michael asked me to look at the dresses he picked out for his five-year-old who was starting kindergarten and then proceeded to tell me about his messy divorce.

Charlie told me he was dealing with trauma from his time in Vietnam.

Neither man was Mr. Right, and I returned home to Indianapolis at the end of the summer. The pink and purple asters were blooming, and the row of bright marigolds in my father's garden was bursting with showers of red and gold. The roses along the fence were still blooming. I owned a little piece of heaven on earth, and my heart was full.

Charlie called after I was back home, but I had moved on. As I hung up the phone from talking with him, my father came in the back door carrying the largest cantaloupe I had ever seen. I watched him set it down on the kitchen counter in front of my mother. "It will taste good for breakfast," he said.

My mother smiled and exclaimed, "My, I can tell already it will be sweet."

Chapter 60
Mrs. Murray

There was only one more week of summer vacation. I sighed, dreading how soon the school year would begin again. I was sitting on the sofa reading the Sunday *Indianapolis Star* from the front page to the end of the ads, as always. I lingered over the classifieds, hoping to discover a bargain. Then my eyes landed on a curious heading: "Mrs. Murray's Dating Service."

> Are you seeking companionship and meaningful connections? Mrs. Murray invites you to explore my personalized dating services where I specialize in matching distinguished singles in the Indianapolis area. Discretion and professionalism assured.

I skipped on and then flipped back. Could I really entertain such a wild idea? The paper slipped into my lap as I closed my eyes. My heart was beating quickly. The summer had changed me, or maybe it was buying the house that gave me a boost of confidence. Or maybe it was simply having my parents' support as I made my own choices for the first time. I picked up the paper and read the ad again.

"Mama," I called to my mother in the kitchen. "Listen to this." I read it aloud. "I'm going to call her. Right now." I knew this wasn't a matter for discussion. If I waited, the impulsive resolution would melt away. A few minutes later, I had an appointment with Mrs. Murray for the next afternoon at one o'clock. It was time for action.

I parked in front of an older apartment building downtown and found myself climbing the worn, wooden stairs to the second floor. Alarm bells were going off in my head. The walls were coated in ancient paint, scruffy from too much contact, and it was hot—steamy hot. Out of breath, I knocked on the dark brown door with "Mrs. Murray" engraved on a small metal plate. I stepped back when I heard someone stirring inside. With my guard up and inching toward the stairs, I watched the door open slowly.

A short woman smiled up at me. Her gray hair with a hint of yellow was tightly permed. Rimless glasses perched low on her nose. She wore a Sunday-go-to-meeting polka-dot dress. I let out my breath and smiled. "I'm Doris Whipple," I said, stepping inside what appeared to be her office.

The afternoon sun slanted through the windows. The air was hot and lifeless. A large wooden table surrounded by a few chairs filled most of the room. Near it sat a wine-colored recliner, Mrs. Murray's easy chair. She gestured toward the table, and I slipped into a chair as she groaned softly, settling into her recliner.

"Well, tell me about yourself," she said.

"I'm a high school teacher. I'm thirty-four."

"Have you ever been married? Do you have children?"

She scribbled notes on a pad. "Well, let me tell you how this works," she said, smiling.

I eyed a black, loose-leaf binder on the table, strikingly similar to the one I had used at the real estate office.

"Open the notebook," she said. Each page featured a black and white photograph of a man, along with a detailed description.

"I assume you'd like to look at the men over thirty." She indicated markers along the side. I flipped to the second section.

"Now, pick out five men you'd like to meet. I'll call them, tell them about you, and give them your phone number. If they're interested, they'll call you."

The photos were all headshots, mostly businessmen in suits and ties. I felt apprehensive. I had never really known a successful businessman outside of education and church.

I turned a page and stopped at a full-length color photograph of a man standing outdoors in what looked like a field. An old wire fence was on one side, and a budding tree stood behind him. He wore blue jeans and a blue shirt. The wind had blown a curl of hair onto his forehead.

I stopped looking. He was the one.

He was 37, a printer at the *Indianapolis Star*. I selected four more men randomly, but Larry Jones was the one who had to call me.

I wrote a check for $50.00. "If this is successful and you marry," Mrs. Murray said, "I'd like an additional $50.00." I wondered how many follow-ups she actually collected.

I left feeling like I had just played the lottery. It was a huge gamble, but I was excited. "Be sure your first meeting is at a coffee shop or public place," she advised as I walked out.

Supper that evening with my parents became a play-by-play of my visit to Mrs. Murray and my new adventure. They didn't have much to say.

The next morning, one of the men called, probably one of the business suit photos. I agreed to meet him that evening outside the movie theater at the mall. I didn't know what to say or how to act when I met my date. Luckily, it was a movie, so small talk was minimal. Was I supposed to hold his hand? I decided to try. He grasped mine tightly and didn't let go. After the movie, we each went to our cars. He said he'd call again soon.

So that was it. I had had my first real date. The next morning, Larry Jones called.

I hadn't written their names down, but I knew it was him. He invited me to lunch at Steak and Ale. I dressed carefully: pink plaid pants and a white blouse with tiny pearl buttons. When the doorbell rang, I jumped up. It was a florist's delivery—a huge bouquet of white and yellow roses from the guy on last night's date. I was still unpacking the flowers when the doorbell rang again.

It was my man in blue jeans, and he was again wearing blue jeans. My smile was big and happy. I saw his little gold Vega in the driveway, but I followed him in my Volkswagen.

It was a lunch date, but food was the last thing on my mind. We tried to chat but stumbled over words. He sounded like I felt—tongue-tied and shy. We focused on our food. I fumbled with my fork and knife, forgetting even how to cut my steak.

Finally, we found a bit of conversation. I told him school would start next week. He told me he'd worked at the *Star* for seventeen years. He paid the bill and asked me out again. I wanted to shout, "Yes! I think you're the one I've been looking for my whole life!" But I just said, "I'd like that."

Chapter 61
Found!

When I got home, I shouted to my mother, "I found him! He's the one!"

"What are you going to do with these flowers?" she asked.

"I'll have to tell that man I won't be seeing him again." Probably holding hands was not a good idea. Then another call came. Men were lining up. I told the next ones I wasn't dating anymore.

Then Mrs. Murray called. "I have a nephew who wants to meet you. Would you please give him a chance?"

"No," I said. "I've already met the man I want to date."

For our second date, Larry and I went to a duck pond in a cemetery. It was my idea. I didn't know much about dating. Squinting and sitting in the hot sun, I turned my head to glance at the man sitting beside me. A breeze rippled his red-brown hair just like his photo. We sat on the bench watching ducks swim.

When it grew monotonous, Larry asked, "Would you like to see my house?"

It would be good to see where he lived. When we turned onto a long, asphalt driveway, I caught my breath. It was a new house. A small tree in the large front yard suggested it had been recently planted.

"Wow, this is beautiful," I said.

We entered through the garage. A green truck was parked there. When he opened the inside door, I was overwhelmed. There was gold shag carpet, and a small chandelier hung over a wrought iron table and chairs. Matching gold appliances were in the kitchen, and there was a window over the sink.

"Would you like to see the rest of the house?" he asked. He showed me the great room with a cathedral ceiling, dark beams, and a brick fireplace with a raised hearth. Then I got a tour of a bathroom, the main bedroom, and another bathroom. Then we sat on his black leather couch.

"It's so beautiful," I said, still dazed. I pointed to some cups in the kitchen. "What are those?"

"I make my own yogurt," he said. We didn't touch. The silence turned awkward. After a few minutes, we went outside. He led me through a vast backyard with over 2 acres. "The barn was here when I bought the land," he said. Inside, baby chicks chirped from a pen.

"Those are my quail," he said.

A black barn cat darted past as we walked back out into the sunshine.

Stepping up on the back deck, he pointed to several small trees. "I got those from my mother's woods." They were maples—my favorite. I could already see them glowing gold and red as autumn approached. Then I saw it, the old wire fence from his photo. And again, my heart confirmed it: This was the man.

On Sunday, Larry's day off, we chose Brown County State Park for our first hike. The trail was rugged. As we slid through fallen leaves on a steep ravine, we caught each other. Shyness melted. We leaned in, and our first kiss locked us together. Our arms wrapped around each other tightly. The hush of the woods with only the sound of whispering leaves surrounded us with peace and reverence. We separated but didn't let go of each other's hands. We kissed again—and again.

I met Larry on August 25. Exactly four weeks later over dinner at a restaurant, he asked me to marry him—again. He had already asked once. I had told him we needed a little more time. But I couldn't sleep that night. I knew. From the moment I saw his picture at Mrs. Murray's, I knew.

He had told me about his job, his family, his habits, his education, and his religious training. He had attended Vacation Bible School a few times at the neighborhood church, and he remembered running in the church basement. I checked that box with a smiley face.

The next evening, in front of his fireplace, I said, "About marrying me . . . let's get married."

We picked out rings the next weekend.

I brought my parents to see his house. "You don't need to worry," I told them. "I'll pay the mortgage on your house. We'll take care of you when you need it."

The last box was checked.

Before I met Larry, I had signed up for a night class at Butler University to finish requirements for my teaching license in Indiana.

"Remember that old road at the edge of the woods by your mother's house?" I asked him. "I have to write a paper for Environmental Conservation. I'm going to write about the forest reclaiming manmade encroachment. Can you take pictures for me over there?"

We found the abandoned road again, its asphalt cracked and disintegrating. The forest was taking it back. I kicked away leaves to reveal weeds and grass. Dandelions and crabgrass were the most prolific, filling the cracks. Mosses crept in, and tangled vines too. Off to the side, blooming alone, was a wild aster.

"Would you take a picture of that?" I asked. As I wrote my paper, I stared at the photo of the flower. Then my mind went back—back to the house in Union Grove one fall day after school. "Mama," I had called. "I have something for you." My arms were full of violet daisies with bright yellow centers.

"Oh!" she had exclaimed. "These are wild asters." She sniffed them and smiled. "I used to pick these in Connecticut." Then she put them carefully in the green Depression glass vase.

The abandoned road was a mirror of my own journey—cracked, crumbling, and broken. But the fears that held me captive were fading. I was ready for a new beginning, bursting with love and hope. I dared to reclaim the dreams of my childhood.

And then, at last . . .

You are invited to share our happiness in the wedding of
Doris E. Whipple and Larry R. Jones
November 20, 1976
Aldersgate Church, Indianapolis

My nephew Gary, wearing a dark blue suit and yellow rose boutonnière ushers you in. The afternoon sun glows through the stained-glass windows. The pastor's wife plays the "Bridal March" on the organ.

Larry's best man stands beside him. Gloria in autumnal orange and my niece Grace in yellow are waiting for me.

Heads turn as I walk down the aisle, arm in arm with my father. My ivory gown, handmade by my mother, is long-sleeved and lace-trimmed. I carry a bouquet of white daisies and yellow roses. My lace veil falls over my shoulders. My eyes are on Larry in a dark blue suit standing at the altar.

Two preachers marry us—the pastor of our church and my brother-in-law, Ed Freymiller. Ed delivers a short, heartfelt message, drawing parallels between love and nature, finishing with the poem "A Thanksgiving" by Lucy Larcom.

Our chosen song, "Green Cathedral" by Gordon Johnstone and Carl Hahn, celebrates our autumnal romance.

I know a green cathedral,
A shadowed forest shrine,
Where leaves in love join hands above
To arch your prayer and mine.

Within its cool depths sacred,
A priestly cedar sighs,
And the fir and pine lift arms divine
Unto the pure blue skies.

In my dear green cathedral
There is a flowered seat,
And choir loft in branched croft
Where songs of bird hymn sweet.

And I like to dream at evening,
When the stars its arches light,
That my Lord and God treads its hallowed sod
In the cool, calm peace of night.
That my Lord and God treads its hallowed sod
In the cool, calm peace of night.

As the last notes fade away, Pastor Denbo rises to perform the vows.

"Larry, wilt thou have this woman to be thy wedded wife, to live together in the holy state of matrimony? Wilt thou love her, comfort her, honor and keep her, in sickness and in health, and forsaking all others, keep thee only unto her so long as ye both shall live?"

"I will."

"Doris, wilt thou have this man to be thy wedded husband, to live together in the holy state of matrimony? Wilt thou love him, comfort him, honor and keep him, in sickness and in health, and forsaking all others, keep thee only unto him so long as ye both shall live?"

"I will."

It's a bright winter day as Larry and I step out of the church. The crisp air stings my cheeks, and I reach for his hand. For the first time, I have someone to brave the storms with me, to keep me warm, to catch me when I fall. This is my new beginning, marked by my choices, our shared dreams, and the quiet power of love.

Epilogue

Life isn't a straight path or a plan you follow. It's a trail you leave behind. I didn't grow up with certainty or clarity, and neither did my sister Linda or any of my other siblings. We were carried along by currents we didn't understand, bound by family and church. But in the end, it wasn't about the plan. It was about spirit, love, survival, and stillness.

We found our way, fragment by fragment, moment by moment. And now, looking back, there was no straight line but only a meandering trail marked by beauty, heartbreak, wonder, and hope.

Linger with me
at the bluebells in the cow pasture,
the oil-slick shimmering with heavenly colors,
the fireworks bursting over the lake,
Shooting stars on a summer night.

And if you find the dead steer in the water,
the snake in the tent,
or even the betrayal of deep trust,
you're still on the way.

And along the way you won't find easy answers or heavenly signs,
But you will find wonder.
Hope beyond crisis,
Your voice reclaimed and rising
The wonder that never lets go,
The quiet, persistent wonder of God.

You'll glimpse it in the first rays of sunrise and the last
blaze of sunset.
You'll find it in the blossoms you stop to smell,
and in the yellow dandelions your children press into your hands.
It's there in the hush beneath trees,
when your fingers brush the branches
and your heart lifts.
And when autumn sets the hills ablaze in reds and golds,
that same wonder will whisper still
of the presence of something vast and sacred,
threaded through sorrow and beauty alike.

Because in the end, there is no plan.
Only the trail that unfolds beneath your feet
And the quiet presence of God beside you all the way.

A 30212 Fountain Spring House, Waukesha, Wis.

Bible School

Left to Right: *Back Row: Floyd Whipple (father), Doris Whipple (mother) holding Linda, Gladys (oldest sister), Muriel (third sister), Gloria (middle sister) /* ***Front Row:*** *Dorie (age three), Floyd Junior*

Myself (age 5), Linda (age 3)

Linda, myself (high school), Gloria

Myself (high school graduation)

Gloria, Myself (going to college)

Gloria, mother, myself, father (college graduation)

Parents 50th anniversary 1975 / ***Left to Right:*** *Gladys, Gloria, myself, father, mother*

Freymiller family at our wedding / ***Left to Right:*** *Gloria, Grace (niece), myself, Larry Jones, Gary (nephew), Ed Freymiller*

Wedding picture, November 20,1975 / Myself and Larry Jones (husband)

About the Author

Doris Jones is the author of Daughter of the Cult, a memoir of survival, resilience, and faith. Born in Connecticut in 1941 as the fifth of six children, she was raised within the strict confines of the Metropolitan Church Association Bible School. After struggling to break free, she earned both her Bachelor's and Master's degrees in Science Education and went on to teach for twenty-five years.

Doris has been married to her husband, Larry, since 1976, and together they have built a life centered on family. They are the proud parents of two children, Sam and Sara, and the delighted grandparents of five. Daughter of the Cult is her debut book, written to give voice to the silenced women like herself and to shed light on the hidden struggles of growing up in a controlling religious community.

Discussion Questions

1. The memoir opens with a vivid scene of childhood in a religious community. How did the author's early environment shape her understanding of love, obedience, and belonging?

2. The title and recurring imagery suggest a search for "the plan." How does this idea evolve from childhood to adulthood? When does the narrator begin to question whether a divine or fixed plan really exists?

3. Family loyalty and faith often conflict in the story. How does the author portray her parents' devotion, and how does that affect the narrator's own faith journey?

4. Many moments in the book center on beauty found in unexpected places—nature, light, animals, or small acts of kindness. How do these moments serve as emotional counterpoints to the surrounding control or hardship?

5. The memoir portrays both individual and communal forms of control. What methods did the church use to enforce conformity? How did the narrator and others find small ways to resist?

6. Memory plays a powerful role in the storytelling. Were there particular scenes that felt dreamlike, symbolic, or especially resonant for you as a reader?

7. The author's voice shifts as she grows older—from childlike innocence to adult reflection. How did those tonal changes affect your experience of the story?

8. The memoir includes difficult scenes of emotional and spiritual abuse. What made those sections bearable—or even healing—to read?

9. Throughout the book, education and reading appear as sources of strength and independence. How does learning become a doorway to freedom?

10. The ending and epilogue suggest that meaning emerges only in hindsight: "no plan, no path, just the trail I leave behind." What does that line mean to you? How does it reframe everything that came before?

11. If you could ask the author one question about her journey, what would it be

www.ingramcontent.com/pod-product-compliance
Lightning Source LLC
LaVergne TN
LVHW010604100826
845148LV00014B/2847

9781684881574